"As both a runner and an at
Lessons learned On the Run
book, I was reminded of what a generous sport running is—we
always get more out of it than we put into it. And the gifts
returned to us through running are multiplied tenfold as we
apply them to other aspects of our personal and work lives."

—Kathleen Bray, JD
Vice President, General Counsel, and Secretary at SFM
Mutual Insurance Company, Minneapolis, Minnesota

"This book inspired me not only to be a better runner but, more
importantly, taught me to see the many life lessons that each
run provides us. David's humorous personal anecdotes about
life and running are a joy to read and provide a thoughtful
challenge on how to live more fully and serve others more
graciously. After reading *Lessons Learned On the Run* my time
running has no longer solely been about how far or fast I could
go but about enjoying the journey, being in the moment and
learning along the paths of life."

—John Donaldson, MBA
Associate Professor, University of Northwestern,
St. Paul, Minnesota

"David is a connector. I've observed him connect with audiences
of my peers as a presenter of continuing education credits. I've
watched his thoughtful introductions of strangers connect
people to forge new relationships. The initial professional
connection we made has developed into valued friendship as

his wisdom has influenced me to connect more deeply with my family, friends, faith and core values. The breadth and depth of the lessons David shares in this book may encourage you to affirm and strengthen these core connections in your life too. Experience his wit and humorous insights as you race through some chapters and slow down to absorb others. Full disclosure. I'm not a runner but this book is so much fun and insightful it almost inspired me to park my road bike and take up running."

—David A. Thesing
CLU, ChFC, CFP-CFO, IFC
National Marketing, Inc., President Bridgeway
Learning Systems, Inc., Coon Rapids, Minnesota

LESSONS LEARNED ON THE **RUN**

A Book About

Running and Life

David Kempston

Lessons Learned on the Run
A Book About Running and Life
© 2020 by David B. Kempston
All rights reserved.

For information, please contact
David B. Kempston (David.Kempston@gmail.com),
8709 Bentwood Drive, Eden Prairie, MN 55344.

First Printing 2020

Paperback ISBN: 978-0-578-23043-6
Ebook ISBN: 978-0-578-23042-9

LCCN: 2017902505

Cover by Francesca Kempston
Edited by Robert Irvin
Interior Design and Typesetting by Josh Pritchard
Author Photograph by Brennan Kempston

TO JOE KEMPSTON

Thank you for sharing your love for running with me—you've taught me much over the years. Thanks also for showing me the way to go. I hope to be like you when I grow up.

ACKNOWLEDGMENTS

I owe the impetus for this book to my youngest son, Connor Kempston. But for his encouragement to take on this project, inertia might have won out. I am thankful for the exhortation—it worked.

I am also indebted to all my fellow runners, past and present. Names might be forgotten, but you left an imprint on me. Your example, encouragement, energy, and tenacious engagement of the elements have inspired me through the decades.

I want to specifically thank Lisa Anderson, Mike Anderson, Cherry Kempston, Brennan Kempston, Shaun Kempston, Tom Mottaz, Bill Walsh, and Jamie Gaboury for listening as I talked through ideas. And thanks for reading chapters and rough drafts. Your patience and feedback have been greatly appreciated. Thanks also to Elle Clauer, Josh Pritchard, Alex Kempston, Francesca Kempston, and my editor, Bob Irvin, for your help with creating the book.

I want to thank my wife, Lisa Kempston for her input, encouragement, and patience during the entire process. I also want to thank my father, Joe Kempston for fostering my lifelong love of running and learning. I've enjoyed our miles together. And of course, I must thank my running buddy. You have been my faithful companion over countless miles. Thank you for your friendship, encouragement, and for putting up with me.

CONTENTS

WHY I RUN

I love to run. Running has been part of my life for more than forty years. Having witnessed three decades of my participation in the sport, my wife has often remarked about the peculiar hold the exercise exerts over me. She's right. I've forged a deep emotional bond with running—one that goes beyond mere fitness. For me, running is also about relationship, connection, and inspiration. The sport embodies life.

Over the years I've run through different seasons and with many people—including five generations of my family. These runs have taught me a great deal. The lessons learned across the miles demonstrate that "More is taught by life than by lip or by lore found in the books of the ages."[1] Simply put, running has been a great life coach.

Running has a great deal of wisdom to share. People learn by doing. We also learn through adversity. Running checks both boxes; it requires effort and endurance. The sport is an excellent teacher because the activity mirrors our experience. The hills and valleys of running reflect the trials and victories of our daily existence. Viewed this way, running is a metaphor for life.

Some say running is about the physical experience and benefit—and that is true. But running is also about

> **Over the years I've run through different seasons and with many people—including five generations of my family.**

our *stories*. In addition to learning through experience, we also learn through narrative. Throughout history, story has been used to teach. Family traditions and histories were orally passed down through the generations. Effective teachers have long employed the technique: Jesus taught with parables; Aesop dispensed wisdom through fables; Abe Lincoln captivated audiences with amusing anecdotes. These days, good speakers still employ compelling illustrations—just watch a popular TED talk.

As a trial lawyer, I'm interested in how a client's story unfolds in the courtroom. I disagree with Detective Friday of *Dragnet*, who wanted "just the facts." Rather, I want to see how those facts fit together to form a compelling narrative. It's about how those elements combine to tell a story—and what we can learn from the shared experience—that interests me.

Sometimes the word "story" carries a bad connotation. We think of embellished exploits, exaggerated fishing tales, or a raconteur who plays loose with the facts. But I'm not referring to tall tales. Rather, I'm talking about true stories: chronicles that instruct. These are the best kind.

As I've talked with others while writing this book, they've become excited and shared their running stories with me. I've had fun listening to why others run and what the sport has taught them. Because running connects and inspires in different ways, each participant has something of value to share. What follows is a collection of my stories about running—and life—and the lessons I've learned along the way.

CHAPTER 1

ALL ARE WELCOME

The sport of running includes people of all sizes, shapes, and abilities. One need not be fast, fit, nor trim to participate—rather, the activity beckons to all who are interested. Like the welcoming Lady Liberty in New York Harbor who greeted many newcomers to a fresh start, the pastime promises a haven for those "huddled masses" yearning for the freedom of the road.[2]

For many participants, running provides a sanctuary that doesn't discriminate. I witnessed this inclusivity on my high school team. Lack a skill set? Then you might as well go out for cross country—the only sport students perform to get in shape for other sports. All are welcome in this venue, where a lack of talent can be offset by the ability to endure. The runner's T-shirt says it well: "My sport is your sport's punishment."

My high school team gave me a place to belong. It provided a common goal and shared experience as I rubbed elbows with a bunch of other skinny fellows who also couldn't get a date for the weekend. Participation helped bridge an awkward adolescent transition because our time was occupied with long runs, two-a-day

> **My high school team gave me a place to belong. It provided a common goal and shared experience as I rubbed elbows with a bunch of other skinny fellows who also couldn't get a date for the weekend.**

workouts, weekly meets, and team get-togethers. Who could ask for more? Cross-country was a welcoming community.

There was a runner on my team who was challenged by a disability. I never knew his diagnosis, but the condition placed him at a disadvantage in high school. A big-boned redhead, he ran with an uneven loping stride and a perpetual smile pasted on his face even when racing. He was cheerful and kind and my cohorts embraced him. He was a good runner who liked to compete. And he ran hard. Although his mental faculties weren't as sharp as those of his teammates, it didn't matter because "As he ran on, he mingled with others."[3]

The camaraderie produced by running extends beyond the confines of a high school team. If you doubt this, spend a morning at a place frequented by runners. You'll see varied demonstrations of mutual respect. One can't help but notice the acknowledgment and encouragement exchanged as runners pass one another.

The sport also produces a deep sense of belonging. This *esprit de corps* is evident at any road race. Before, during, and after the event, participants greet, encourage, and extol their fellows.

The sport provides opportunities for all—mile relays, 5Ks, 10Ks, half marathons, full marathons, ultras, team relays, masters track meets, trail runs, and mudders abound. These forums feature athletes who span the spectrum from elite to novice, fit to fat, and serious to silly.

You can pick your event or mix and match. No one size fits all.

Running doesn't discriminate due to age, either. I ran as a child, as a young man, and now I run as a grandpa. I'm not alone. My father has run into his late seventies. There are those who have continued to run into their nineties!

Granted, one may need to modify pace, stride, and frequency (perhaps switching to a "periodic trundle," as a friend nearing retirement likes to say), but barring injury running remains a welcoming host who always extends a gracious invitation. So grab a pair of shoes and join in.

CHAPTER 2

RUNNING IS A HAPPY PLACE

In busy, modern life, we all need a place of refuge, a safe place. A happy place. It doesn't need to be a physical location; rather, it can be an activity, something that restores the soul.

I'm not assuming an abstract philosophical stance. This is a real, practical point that many disregard to their detriment. It's important to recharge your batteries regularly—regardless of your power source. Failure to do so can lead to misery.

I learned this lesson as a young, stressed, and overworked attorney with three small children. I was doing too many different things and wasn't taking time to tend to myself. As a result, all aspects of my life were affected. Physically, psychologically, spiritually—I was in bad shape.

Deciding to be proactive, I made a short list of activities I used to do that brought me joy. Reviewing the compilation, I decided to reengage in refreshment. One item on my list was running. I'd taken a break from the sport. I'd run intermittently in the years after high school but hadn't maintained consistency.

But even that small amount of running disappeared during my first years of practice as I struggled to survive in litigation. I realized change was required. Following that epiphany, I began to run again—along with gradually adding other items from my healthy to-do list into my routine. The infusion of activity helped. I slowly restored balance to my life. And this was good.

The American Bar Association has published a study on the state of lawyers' health, concluding that, "to be a good lawyer, you have to be a healthy lawyer."[4] This conclusion applies to all vocations, and it's not a novel concept. An elder statesman from a different era recognized that "to be really happy and really safe, one ought to have at least two or three hobbies, and they must all be real."[5] This busy fellow was right. His observation from yesteryear applies today. His name? Winston Churchill.

Everybody needs a happy place. Running has become my happy place. In saying that, I don't mean I always experience euphoria when I run—but, overall, the sport has become a place of sanctuary, reflection, and inspiration.

To quote a memorable line by British sprinter Eric Liddell in the movie *Chariots of Fire*, "When I run, I feel God's pleasure."[6] This statement resonates with me. Running provides me great pleasure. Going a step further, I've often said that running is cheaper than a psychiatrist. Joking aside, that is true. The activity functions like a Greek drama in my life, promoting catharsis and purging unhealthy emotions as I pound the pavement.

I'm not saying every run will make you happy. Much has been written about the runner's high and what happens when your endorphins kick in. As noted by Dr. Tim Noakes: "The current feeling is that endorphins may play a role in the runner's high, but probably do not alter pain perception during exercise."[7] This famed emotional high can be elusive, and you probably won't find it on every outing.

But it does happen.

When the runner's high hits me, I become giddy. My running buddy says it's easy to identify because I turn into "the Chihuahua." Morphing into a yappy, prancing, and cavorting canine-like runner occurs infrequently, but that's OK. I'm interested in the overall, long-term effects of running, and these include improved health, a sense of well-being, and a temporary escape from life's pressures. These are benefits worth pursuing.

Running may not result in your renewal and restoration. I recognize that all people are different. Many of my non-runner friends can't relate to my attachment to the sport. That's fine. But you need something— some place, some activity—that makes you happy. And by that I don't mean escaping your life periodically by going to the grocery store, as suggested to a lawyer friend of mine by her grinning spouse as she headed off for her weekly trip to the grocery, list in hand. Although shopping provided a respite from demanding clients and cranky children, my friend will tell you that getting groceries doesn't refresh her spirit on a deep level.

> **Many of my non-runner friends can't relate to my attachment to the sport. That's fine. But you need something— some place, some activity—that makes you happy.**

Rather, I'm talking about something disconnected from your daily obligations and responsibilities. If you don't have a regular activity that recharges your batteries, consider finding one. Having a healthy hobby and reprising it regularly will do wonders for your spirit.

I don't want to overstate my case. Running probably won't save your life. It's not going to turn you into a fantastic person, and it won't solve your relationship problems.

But it can be useful. And it might make you happier.

CHAPTER 3

YOU MUST START SOMEWHERE

Beginning to run can be difficult. Whether due to injury, inactivity, or lack of time, it's hard to overcome inertia. Injuries or busyness can sideline us. At other times, the gravitational pull of the couch can be forceful. And when we do begin to run, those first few steps—especially the ones out the door—are often the most difficult. But as with all things in life, regardless of our circumstances, we've got to start somewhere.

According to an old Chinese proverb, "The journey of a thousand miles begins with a single step." My family was reminded of this truth a few years back when we embarked on a medical odyssey with our daughter. One week after she graduated from college, Kate sustained a catastrophic brain injury. As a result, she was in a coma for about two weeks. Following the injury, my wife and I spent nine long days at her bedside in Mississippi, then flew her back home to Minnesota on an air ambulance. Kate gradually came out of her coma and spent the following months in various medical facilities.

As she recovered, she was initially quite disabled. She had to learn how to walk, talk, and eat all over again. The process was tedious. When she first began walking again, she took baby steps. Her treatment included extensive therapy with multiple modalities. As she progressed, running was added to her regimen. Although she'd occasionally run before her injury, she never enjoyed it.

Kate's injury didn't improve her perspective on running. If anything, it made it worse. Getting harnessed in and forced to run on a treadmill, when it was hard enough to walk, was a frightening experience. My daughter has never been afraid of much. Her friends claim she's not afraid of anything. However, on that first morning when the therapist strapped her into the treadmill and made her run, she was terrified. What followed were a few pained steps with a very altered gait. It was hard to watch.

But . . . Kate did it. She took those first difficult steps. Since then she's gone on to a remarkable recovery. Some deficits remain, but her healing has been miraculous. And running on that dreaded treadmill helped. But she didn't start out running. Instead, Kate's journey toward motion began with a small first step that later progressed to a run.

Unlike my daughter, I like to run, and I do so when able. When other people learn this, many confide they'd also like to take up running. They often follow with an admission that they either don't know what to do or don't have time to do it. As an attorney, I'm surrounded by busy people. My peers love to complain about how much they work or how busy they are. It's a recurring theme. And busyness isn't limited to the lawyer world. Everyone is busy. That said, we all have time to do what is important to us—within reason. It's a matter of choice and priority.

Like Kate, if you want to begin moving, you've got to start somewhere. And there is no time like the present. With running, there is no set timetable. Everyone is different. A lawyer I know ran his fiftieth marathon right around his fiftieth birthday. Other runners I know began running later in life. I recently read about someone who ran fifty marathons after turning 50! My point? *Start where you are.*

The idea is to get moving. Ask Kate—motion is lotion.

When you do start moving, be wise. Keep in mind the musical refrain from *The Sound of Music*: "Start at the very beginning. It's a very good place to start."[8] Beginners sometimes attempt a training schedule that would frustrate an Olympian. Don't do that. Be realistic. Chart a course you can follow. If you haven't done anything in a long time, start slowly. Like Kate, you may

> **I recently read about someone who ran fifty marathons after turning 50! My point? *Start where you are.***

need to take baby steps at first. Begin with walking. After that, alternate between jogging and walking. Depending on how it goes, you can slowly progress to running.

Don't be like my friend, an erstwhile Nordic ski jumper, who used to go on very long runs—three decades ago. Recently he decided to begin running again; his first effort was a 40-minute trot. He overdid it. Afterward, he paid the price.

When asked why he began so briskly, my friend responded, "Because that's what I used to do." Overall, he's a wise fellow; however, he placed his prudence on the shelf that morning. Learn from his mistake. Be aware of your physical condition and act accordingly. Overdoing it will lead to injury or discouragement. And if you get discouraged, your new resolve will fizzle out.

The goal is to develop a routine you'll use regularly. As author Gretchen Rubin noted in *Better Than Before*, "The more consistently [we] perform an action, the more automatic it becomes, and the fewer decisions it requires[.]"[9]

Remember—and this is true with all choices you make—it takes time to develop a habit.

But you've got to start somewhere.

CHAPTER 4

DIFFERENT-SIZED CONTAINERS

In high school, I ran cross-country for the Mead Panthers. The team had a storied running tradition. During my junior year our top athlete won the state meet. I wasn't at his level. In fact, I was quite average. I typically ran number seven (last member) on varsity or as number one on junior varsity.

Our team was large, and our harriers possessed a wide range of ability. Some seemed born to run. Others did not. Our coach appreciated talent, but he encouraged, expected, and respected hard work. He used to say God gave each runner a different-sized container but left it up to us as to how much we would fill it. By container, he meant talent. And by fill, he meant how much we got out of our natural ability. He was right. We can't change our starting point, but how far we go with what we've got depends largely on effort.

During high school I saw this truth play out many times. Through hard work and perseverance, less talented runners improved and performed at increasingly higher levels over the course of a season. In contrast, more gifted runners who didn't work as hard didn't improve as much—or perhaps failed to progress at all. As a wise teacher once observed, "The fastest runner doesn't always win the race."[10]

The container concept cemented in my mind as I watched a season play out for two top runners. I'll call them Dan and Darren. Their story underscores talent versus determination. To paraphrase Coach, Dan had a small container, but he crammed it full. He also drove an orange Pinto. When not sporting about in his cool car, he ran sixty-plus miles per week year-round. This high mileage allowed him to compete at a high level—he consistently ran number one or two on the team.

By contrast, Darren possessed a huge container, but he never worked out in the off-season. Instead, he ran off talent. Toward the end of each season he would finally catch and then eclipse the frustrated Dan because, by then, Darren had partially filled his supersized container.

The container concept isn't limited to running. It applies to all aspects of life. I took this paradigm to college with me and worked hard. To quote Coach, I filled my container. After graduating from college, I succumbed to the siren call of law school. There, just like on my high school team, I was surrounded by a wide divergence of talent and ability. Over the semesters, however, the smartest students didn't always come out on top. Instead, diligence and determination dictated outcome. That's because innate intelligence only goes so far in academics. At some point, you have to roll up your sleeves and do the work. As Hemingway noted, if you want to succeed, then "Work every day. No matter what has happened the day or night before, get up and bite on the nail."[11]

> Over the semesters, however, the smartest students didn't always come out on top. Instead, diligence and determination dictated outcome.

This truth was demonstrated again when I entered the practice of law. When I began working as an attorney at a Minneapolis firm, I doubted my ability. I confessed this fear to my father. Reinforcing the container concept, he told me that people succeed if they are:

- smart enough,
- honest, and
- work hard.

This sage counsel proved accurate. Over the years I've noticed that the most naturally gifted attorneys don't always rise to the top. Instead, just like the runners on my cross-country team, those who combine talent with diligence and daily bite the nail—these lawyers tend to perform at the highest level.

The container concept is a great equalizer. The most accurate measure of success looks not just at rank or place of finish; rather, it assesses what you did with what you were given. We hold in higher esteem those achievers who, through hard work and determination, accomplish more than those who coast on talent.

Regardless of our starting point, may we all seek to fill our containers to the brim. To borrow a phrase my brother loves to use: "Maximize what you got."

CHAPTER 5

EVERY RUN IS A GIFT

Every run is a gift. This lesson hit home when I ran three miles with my 77-year-old dad. It was January, and ice and snow covered the ground. He came to town to perform my daughter's wedding. We experienced a wonderful week together. Our winter run punctuated a fun time of family connection.

Years ago, I married an Iowan right after college and then moved to Minnesota to attend law school. After passing the bar exam, I stayed on the frozen tundra. My parents remained on the west coast and, for the last three decades, we have seen each other only once or twice a year. I see my siblings even less. These infrequent visits provide needed catch-ups.

On this January run, as Dad and I picked our way around a sheltered loop, I pointed out the ice and gave advice on navigating the trail. We've logged a lot of miles together over the years and through a variety of seasons, but I can't recall another run where I was so conscious of his presence. Part of it was concern about the ice, but the other part was pure enjoyment. This was a special run for me—it wasn't mystical, but it was delightful to run with him and think of all the changes over the years. I'd run with him as a child and, as of this ice-snared run, I had two grandchildren and another soon to arrive. How many grandparents get to run with their own parent? Not many.

Who knows how many more runs there will be with my dad? Our outdoor excursion reminded me that each run is a bonus. I was coming off a season filled with injury and hadn't run much in the preceding year. It felt good to tromp the trail with my pop. I relished every minute.

I wasn't only basking in quality time with Dad—I was also enjoying the physical act of motion again after having been sidelined and not able to run the previous year. During that span I often wondered if I'd ever run again.

> **Who knows how many more runs there will be with my dad? Our outdoor excursion reminded me that each run is a bonus.**

Running used to be an obligation—something I felt compelled to do. Runs were to be endured. Yes, I appreciated the benefits, but not the process. That has changed. The attitude shift is a function of both age and injury because, with age, I've endured extended seasons where I couldn't run. I missed it terribly during those times. The older I get, the more I prize the sport. I realize I won't be able to run forever. This too shall pass. That makes each outing a gift to be savored. Each run is unique. It's a chance to indulge my flesh. The activity makes me grateful.

Gratitude reminds me of my mother-in-law. She possessed the gift of enjoying the present moment. She could squeeze tremendous joy out of life's mundane minutes. A phenomenal performer in her youth, in her later years she often broke out in spontaneous dance. An inch shy of five feet, this diminutive dancer's influence outsized her stature. She placed a sign at the family lake that read, "Each day is a gift. That's why they call it the present." The placard was a great reminder. She lived those words and we benefited from her example.

Her life was cut short by complications from cancer and radiation therapy. It was a tragic end to a good life. She is missed. So is her spontaneity. Her ability to fully enjoy the moment is rare. So many people are mired in the past or waiting expectantly for the future—with the result that they can't enjoy the present. Instead, they simply endure, longing for change.

That is a sad place to be.

Running reminds me that life itself is a gift. Like a run, each day provides an opportunity to enjoy the world around us. And like a run, each day passes quickly. Life is indeed a vapor.[12] We don't know when it will end. So stop waiting for a future time when you think you'll be happy. Put off the endurance mentality. Instead, fully engage in the *now*. You've been given one life to live—embrace it.

> **Running used to be an obligation—something I felt compelled to do. Runs were to be endured. Yes, I appreciated the benefits, but not the process. That has changed.**

CHAPTER 6

WORDS MATTER

As children we all learned the nursery rhyme "Sticks and stones may break my bones, but words will never hurt me." Unfortunately, this familiar line isn't true. Statements—whether spoken out loud by others or silently by ourselves—can wield profound influence.

As a high school runner, I was inconsistent. I'd run a good race, followed by a bad race, followed by a good race. You get the idea. This inconsistency frustrated my coach. He commented on this failing several times during our years together. I still remember him declaring, after a particularly poor performance, "I finally figured it out—you're afraid to succeed."

At the time, the words took me aback. I wondered if they were true. Too much time was spent ruminating on the message. The proclamation echoed in my head for many years afterward. Eventually it receded.

As a middle-aged lawyer who has heard many foolish statements, I look back now and chuckle at the long-ago comment. It was the excited utterance of a frustrated coach who was caught up in the moment. His words weren't prophetic. I've learned over time that I'm not afraid to succeed—in running or otherwise.

Coach could've been more circumspect. He didn't need to say those words. His lament was ironic because he's one of the first people who taught me about self-talk. I'd never heard of the concept before joining his team. He was a big proponent of positive self-talk. He'd regularly remind his runners of the importance of our inner monologue throughout the season. He encouraged us to listen to ourselves and change our negative thoughts and input. This was useful instruction. It's unfortunate that he didn't consistently embrace the self-evident corollary, namely, "positive coach talk."

At the time, I thought self-talk was just a euphemism for ignoring pain. I failed to make the connection between positive self-talk and negative emotions. I've since learned that emotional people (like me) often let feelings dictate thought life and mood. Thus, if we feel or think poorly, we assume life must be bad. However, emotions aren't necessarily accurate indicators.

> **It takes diligence to recognize a negative idea and replace it with truth. With effort, however, we can change bad mental habits.**

Negative sentiments don't need to lead to damaging self-thoughts or destructive self-talk. Instead, it's important to tell ourselves the truth. This is not a one-time occurrence—we all need constant self-reminders regarding truth. It took me a long time to figure this out.

Uninvited notions do enter our minds. When they do, it's useful to heed the words of Martin Luther, who said, "While I can't stop the birds from flying over my head, I can keep them from building nests in my hair." This is good advice. When the negative thoughts come to roost in our mind, we need to drive them out and replace them with truth.

Condemning thoughts and adverse self-talk need not control us. If we discipline our thoughts, we can retrain how we talk to ourselves. It takes diligence to recognize a negative idea and replace it with truth. With effort, however, we can change bad mental habits.

Please note, I'm not referring to self-reflection or self-correction. Everyone needs to do both. Rather, I'm talking about combating the negative thoughts and poor self-talk that can otherwise dominate us.

Coach taught me a lot about the influence of words—whether uttered by others or spoken to self. Still, he missed a teachable moment after my lousy race that day. Words pack a lot of power. We need to be careful how we use them—especially when speaking from a position of influence. We should guard our mouths and watch how we speak to others and ourselves. For as a wise teacher once warned, "Life and death are in the power of the tongue and those who love it will eat its fruit."[13]

Let's sow life with our speech. May we use our words to encourage others and convey truth.

CHAPTER 7

NO SUCH THING AS BAD WEATHER

T. S. Eliot once wrote that April is the cruelest month.[14] Clearly, he never visited Minnesota in January. Eliot was speaking about more than just weather, but teasing aside, he was on to something. Winter running in the upper Midwest can be brutal. As a transplant who has now resided in America's thirty-second state for about as many years, I'm still amazed at how the topic of weather dominates conversation among the frozen chosen. If it weren't for the weather, Minnesotans might not have much to say.

Winters in Minnesota are long and tend to drive people indoors. The harsh weather can result in cabin fever or, worse, depression. In my middle years, I've increasingly sought to redeem the long cold season by running, snowboarding, skiing, and walking the dog, with the result that I spend a lot of time outside in the elements. Treadmills are to be avoided. During the 2019 "polar vortex," for instance, I ran a 5K outside when it was -29 degrees. I do relish being outdoors in the winter.

> I'm still amazed at how the topic of weather dominates conversation among the frozen chosen. If it weren't for the weather, Minnesotans might not have much to say.

Recently, an old college friend from San Francisco came to town. He'd been to every state in the union but one. That would be North Dakota. To resolve his deficiency, on a whim, we took a short road trip to North Dakota in mid-January. It was -13 degrees as we strolled through downtown Fargo looking for a restaurant. I froze. The situation was ironic: the Californian was warm and the Minnesotan cold.

We had fun that night in Fargo. We ate at a great little brewery—and even peeked in on a local winter festival known as Frostival. My friend was warm because I'd spent time getting him ready and loaned him suitable clothes to wear in the bitter cold weather—Dale sweater, turtleneck, wind-stopper headband, and good mittens. But I failed to make sure I dressed properly. Like I said, I froze. He even made fun of me at one point since I'm a winter-lover.

The next day I ran 8.5 miles in -7 degrees. I was dressed appropriately. I wasn't cold. My point? Just ask the Norwegians, who will tell you, "There is no bad weather, just inadequate clothing."

Adequate clothing makes all the difference. Years ago my running buddy and I went for a winter ten-miler that included a loop around a well-traveled Minneapolis urban lake. It was a cold day with the temperature hovering around zero. And there was an ill wind blowing from the north. Before leaving the house, my companion made a poor decision when he rejected nylon running pants in favor of a cotton pair. A fateful choice.

As we traversed the northeast side of the lake, an arctic breeze blasted us—hard. Gusting up to 20 miles per hour, it made for miserable running. We were about four miles out when my friend began to complain. After another mile going straight into the wind, the complaints assumed an urgent tone. His family jewels were freezing, and he was worried. There wasn't much we could do since we were about five miles from home. Given the worsening nature of his clothing crisis, we tried to brainstorm a solution on the run. To misquote Dickens, "These were [not] the best of times."[15] We didn't have great expectations.

The far end of this lake is peppered with garbage cans. I sprinted ahead and began rummaging through the refuse containers in hopes of finding some material adequate for blocking the wind. Given the time of year, the contents were sparse. All I could find were used dog poop bags. Frostbite notwithstanding, my running buddy declined the proffered solution. Leaning into the last available trash can, I triumphantly retrieved a large, empty, plastic shopping bag. He snatched that sack out of my hands and swiftly thrust it down the front of his cotton pants. It did the trick.

> Just ask the Norwegians, who will tell you, "There is no bad weather, just inadequate clothing."

Having narrowly averted disaster, we rounded the north end of the lake and allowed the wind to help push us home. Within a short time, my friend announced that the bulky bag stuffed in his crotch and the change in the wind direction had combined to produce great relief.

That run was a painful reminder of the dangers of inadequate clothing. Our dumpster-diving adventure also underscored that nylon cuts through a cold headwind much better than its cotton counterpart. As I like to say, "Pants are an important part of preparation."[16]

CHAPTER 8

DEBT ISN'T YOUR FRIEND

All runners are familiar with oxygen debt. The dictionary defines the condition this way: "A cumulative deficit of oxygen available for oxidative metabolism that develops during periods of intense bodily activity and must be made good when the body returns to rest."[17] This wordy explanation falls short. It fails to convey both the feeling and impact of this dilemma.

My coach used to describe this condition as feeling like a bear jumped on your back. Writer Neal Bascomb captured this beastly quality in his description of Sir Roger Bannister just after breaking the four-minute mile barrier in May 1954.

> Bannister was barely conscious and was overwhelmed with pain. For a moment, he could see only in black and white. His system was completely taxed from lack of oxygen. His legs and arms felt as if someone were gripping them tightly.[18]

Ouch. Regardless of how you define it, oxygen debt hurts.

In my mid-thirties I raced a 5K on Father's Day. It had been a long time since my last race, and I had no idea what to expect. Swept up by the excitement, I went out briskly and tucked in behind the race leaders. My first mile split was much faster than anything I'd run in a long time.

The pace was simply too swift.

It was an out-and-back race, and the bill for my indiscretion came due at the halfway mark. The bear had landed squarely on my back. Soon my legs turned into tree trunks, and I began to experience tunnel vision. I faded rapidly. It felt as if someone had tied paint cans to each arm as I struggled to get to the finish. I even stumbled into the curb a few times in the last half mile. Several runners passed me as I ran out of gas. It was an ignominious finish.

As I later recounted to a group of friends my experience of going out too fast and blowing up, my running buddy asked, incredulously, "What were you trying to do? Did you really think you were going to win the race?" The others chuckled at his rhetoric.

In retrospect, it would've been helpful if he'd asked me those questions before I raced myself into unforgivable debt. Perhaps then I'd have constrained myself and conserved equity at the outset. But at the time, I really wasn't thinking. I was too busy running. Heedless of the consequences, I went out too fast, went too deeply into debt, and blew up.

There is a life lesson here. Debt isn't your friend. This is a useful concept to live by. Granted, there are different kinds of debt. Moderate debt can be useful, and our society rests squarely on the concept of consumer debt. That said, we are wise to heed the admonition of Thomas Stanley, who reminded us, "Whatever your income, always live below your means."[19] Sage words to live by. When the economy soured in late 2007, I saw several clients go under because once their cash flow slowed, they couldn't service their debt.

> **I was too busy running. Heedless of the consequences, I went out too fast, went too deeply into debt, and blew up.**

Over the years I've mentored many students at local law schools. Some of my mentees incurred substantial debt to finance their education. I've watched the trend of increasing student loans with concern. These loans are easy to obtain. In some ways these young debtors remind me of that race on Father's Day, as these lawyers-to-be don't recognize the danger of their debt.

It's surprising how much debt can accumulate in three short years. In some cases, law school loans are added to prior undergrad obligations. The significant debt accrued by some law students then becomes an anchor that can weigh them down for a lifetime. This burden has a far-reaching effect. It can affect career and family decisions for years. Once acquired, it's not easily undone.

Debt doesn't respect occupation or age. A successful surgeon I know got out over the front of his financial skis in his sixties and eventually declared bankruptcy. His circumstances changed drastically and, as a result, he continued working well past his intended retirement date.

Beware: debt can crush you. It can also disrupt and obstruct, keeping you from getting where you want to go. It weighs you down. Be careful about going into debt when running, purchasing, or borrowing—there will always be consequences.

CHAPTER 9
SPIT HAPPENS

Runners like to spit. This is a habit my nonrunner friends find irksome. It's difficult to explain the runner's urge to spit to someone who lacks the experience. The cultural chasm is hard to bridge. Finding the correct verbiage to convey the sentiment is difficult. Talking about expectoration or expelling bodily fluids doesn't help.

For runners, the need to spit often occurs more frequently on a hot day. This seems counterintuitive because running in hot weather should promote conservation of hydration, right? Alas, I cannot explain this one; however, I will admit that I also spit on cold runs. It's a fact—spit happens. And sometimes the consequences are unexpected.

Early in my junior year of high school cross-country, Coach loaded us up in the back of his rusty pickup truck and hauled us out into the country to drop us off for a longer run. I suspect that's not legal anymore, but at the time, stuffing a dozen teenage boys in the back of a truck didn't register any complaints. The intent was to drop us off about ten miles from school so we could get a nice rolling hill run on the way back.

Situated on the outside back of the pickup bed, face into the wind, I was daydreaming, enjoying the rest before the run. Lost in thought, I was rudely brought to my senses when a large loogey struck me squarely in the face. This was a big one. And it was quite viscous.

It turns out one of my teammates, a younger runner, standing up front, had cleared his throat and spat off the side of the truck, thinking it would clear. He was wrong. It did not. And just like that, my face became his spittoon.

As I wiped the goo off my face with my hand, I heard my truckmates murmur and then break into laughter. Curt, the source of the spit, looked chagrined. We were separated by several scrawny, puerile running bodies, and we were traveling in the back of a truck, so there was no way to effectively communicate. Our spectators anticipated a fight.

It's fair to say that spitting is gross. The sound and sight of the activity often provokes frowns from onlookers. And in many cultures, spitting on another person is a sign of shame. I can still recall recoiling in disgust when my mom spat on a handkerchief to wipe grime off my 5-year-old face at some long-ago church function.

These thoughts and a few more raced through my mind as I stood, wet-faced, in the back of that truck. As I cleaned up, I collected myself.

Who knew that an errant ejection of bodily fluid could lead to such a great result?

When we reached the drop-off point, Curt came over and quickly apologized. He thought I'd be angry. He explained the failed attempt to clear the truck. I accepted the apology and then laughed. He laughed back.

That chance encounter cemented a lifelong friendship. After the apology, Curt and I struck up a conversation as we ran back to school together. We ended up becoming fast friends. In the years that followed, we shared lots of adventures and ran many miles together.

Curt was the best man in my wedding. We've maintained a friendship all the way to our fifties even though we're now separated by several states. Who knew that an errant ejection of bodily fluid could lead to such a great result?

Like I said, spit happens. It can even hit you in the face unexpectedly. When it does, collect your thoughts, clear your face—and expect good things.

CHAPTER 10

NOBODY CARES ABOUT YOUR WORKOUT

I'm sorry, but nobody cares about your workout. You do, but that's it. OK, maybe a few people care—your workout buddy, your mom, and perhaps the alpha dog who's trying to one-up you. Those excepted, most people don't care. So please don't inflict your workout news on others.

Runners love to run. They get excited about the topic. Just ask one and they'll gladly share their enthusiasm. Ever notice how a casual conversation about weekend activities with a runner can turn into a lengthy monologue about a ten-mile jaunt? Intensity, heart rate, and the weather may mingle in as the storyteller gets lost in minute details. Many runners are guilty of this crime.

These types blow by civil niceties and go straight to the intended topic—themselves. Often there is no pretense of conversational give and take.

We've all encountered talkative exercise buffs who loudly proclaim their latest running exploits—or, worse yet, the painful details of their diet and sleep patterns. These types blow by civil niceties and go straight to the intended topic—themselves. Often there is no pretense of conversational give and take.

Other runners are more skilled at pontificating about their physical prowess. These sorts set traps for the unwary. They employ the setup question. The snare may appear as a friendly inquiry, like, "What did you do on Saturday morning?" Or, "Have you ever run a marathon?" And if they find out you ran a marathon, they invariably ask this one: "What was your time?"

To the uninitiated, these questions seem innocent. Bite on one, however, and the hook is set. Often, before you've even finished your response, the questioner launches into the dreaded details of their most recent athletic accomplishment. You're then stuck on the receiving end of a lengthy word dump. What follows is no fun.

This malady isn't limited to the running world. Crossfitters are also prone to the crime of exercise-brag. Moving beyond the fitness realm, many people seem to share this common trait— the inability to listen without talking about themselves. We've all encountered bloviators. They kill conversation. To misquote a fun book, "[Their words] took mine away."[20] This observation is both sad and true.

You've likely noticed this trait in certain friends or acquaintances. The bulk of the communication in these relationships consists of a one-sided dialogue. You must set aside blocks of time to absorb the deluge of information that will inevitably come your way during the forty-five-minute conversation with this verbal monopolizer. In the vernacular, it's shut-up-and-listen-to-me time. This one-sided banter is exhausting.

> **To the uninitiated, these questions seem innocent. Bite on one, however, and the hook is set.**

Granted, it can be easy to talk about ourselves and the causes that are important to us. But we need to fight this temptation. Most people entertain at least one ardent interest. However, passions are variegated, not universal. We need to understand an audience may not appreciate our ardor. We're wise to heed the admonition, "The prudent keep their knowledge to themselves, but a fool's heart blurts out folly."[21] Seek to be aware of others in conversation.

My dad says there are two types of people in the world: those who enter a crowded room and say, "Look, world, here I am"; and those who enter the same room and say, "Hey, you, there you are." Perhaps my pop oversimplifies human nature, but he provides a good reminder. We should strive to be better listeners. As the Bard put it, "Give every man thy ear, but few thy voice[.]"[22]

Please note, I'm not talking about occasional overindulgence in storytelling. We all love a good story. A periodic heartfelt gush about an exciting event is fine. But repeated, self-focused soliloquies are not. Remember, it's how one is characterized that counts.

Being a good listener is a skill we can improve with practice. Improvement requires awareness, self-control, and discipline— three qualities possessed by most diligent runners. If we can bring these attributes to bear in a consistent manner on our physical state, it follows that we can do the same with our mental state. The results merit the effort.

CHAPTER 11
BUY GOOD SHOES

Shoes are important. This is true for running and beyond. I remember being told in law school that the first thing a jury looks at are the lawyer's shoes. The professor had a point: footwear can make an important first impression, a helpful reminder that the proper tool is essential for a job. As a trial lawyer who's since spent a lot of time litigating, I'll attest that proper courtroom attire includes an attractive pair of dress shoes.

I've grown to love good dress shoes; my favorites are Allen Edmonds. They're comfortable, classy, and a bit on the spendy side. The cork insoles form to your feet with wear. These well-built Wisconsin-made beauties will travel many miles with proper care. Like all footwear, they last longer if you don't wear the same pair every day. Swap them out. And once they're worn down, you can get them recrafted.

Allen Edmonds are well worth the cost if you need quality dress shoes. I own several. I keep them in the back of my car, in their original boxes, stored in soft felt bags and reinforced with cedar trees. I do change them frequently. One time, as I was doing so, a friend peered into the back of my car and casually inquired whether I was operating a mobile shoe store. I had to admit, it did look that way. Oh well, when the shoe fits . . .

Over time, I've learned that quality footwear is worth the investment. I didn't always know this, however.

I won't say the name, but in the early 1980s, when a now-defunct brand was trying to break into the running gear market, Dad and I got hoodwinked. A family acquaintance who had a part-time gig as a shoe representative knew that my father liked to run. In what I assume she thought was a generous overture, she offered to comp Dad a pair of new running shoes.

Being a good provider and flattering himself as thrifty—or sensing an opportunity to double his value—my father inquired if his son, who also enjoyed running, could likewise obtain a free pair. Yes, he was told, that would happen. Dad and I were quite excited about the windfall. Bewitched, perhaps, is a better descriptor. We waited with bated breath for the promised freebies to arrive. We waited and waited and waited. When we'd finally forgotten about them—and this was a hint we should've left well enough alone—they arrived.

> **Heedless of the danger, we doubled down and put more miles on them instead of placing them in the trash—where they belonged in the first place.**

We tore open our matching boxes with palpable excitement. Our enthusiasm was misplaced. First, the shoes were ugly: they were purplish in color. Next, they were off in their proportions. We should've heeded the aesthetic alarms and stopped there. For as is often the case in life, function follows form. These weren't good shoes.

Uncomfortable at the outset, they aged prematurely. Heedless of the danger, we doubled down and put more miles on them instead of placing them in the trash—where they belonged in the first place. Because of our thrift and shared stubborn nature, we both developed foot problems. Younger and more elastic, I recovered more rapidly than my elder. Independent of one another, we eventually gave up and got new shoes.

Bouncing back from our bad shoe debacle, we both learned a valuable lesson. Don't run in bad shoes. Don't run in worn-out shoes either. Instead, buy good shoes. Confirm the fit. Make sure the last is built to your stride. Change them out frequently. Get rid of them sooner than you need to. Better yet, mimic my running buddy and have two or three pair—or, in his case, perhaps ten pair—that you rotate through on a regular basis. And do keep track of the mileage and length of time since you first ran in them.

> **Better yet, mimic my running buddy and have two or three pair—or, in his case, perhaps ten pair—that you rotate through on a regular basis.**

Remember, running shoes, even expensive ones, are a lot cheaper than copays to a foot doctor or physical therapist. If nothing else, preserving your feet, so you can run without injury, will save you money in the long run. Consider: if you're injured, then you may go out to eat, to the movies, or bored-shopping to fill up your spare time now that you can't go for your usual weekend runs.

It's OK to be thrifty, but don't be cheap. In my younger lawyer years, an older partner used to remind me to avoid being "pennywise and pound foolish" when defending lawsuits. His sage advice applied to more than litigation. Whatever you're doing, it's worthwhile to spend money on good products. As with all things in life, you tend to get what you pay for.

In the long run, buying quality shoes constitutes a worthwhile investment. Your feet will thank you.

Plus, you'll get the periodic joy of running in a new pair of shoes.

CHAPTER 12

AT THE END, ALL YOU NEED IS A BAG

When you run a point-to-point race, you need a way to get your stuff to the finish line. Most race organizers will provide you with a plastic bag in which you can place your warmups and the other items that you can't carry during the event. That bag then gets delivered to your destination while you're running the race. At the end, all you need is your bag.

The race bag doesn't hold much. It doesn't need to. At the end of a race, you don't need a whole lot of stuff. There's a good lesson here—a truth made apparent toward the end of my grandfather's life.

As a youngster, I spent a lot of time with my mom's father. He was born in Canada, the only son of a British immigrant. A product of the Great Depression, Grandpa grew up laboring long hours in his father's bakery. This man knew hard work. Emigrating to California at age 40 with his wife and two young daughters, he made a good life for himself in the United States. Grandpa could fix anything. Holding a variety of jobs over his life, he ultimately became a math teacher and tennis coach.

He was smart, quirky, socially awkward, and generous. He modeled virtue and diligence, and I often toiled alongside him as a teenager at the apartment complex he owned and operated. As the saying goes, "More is caught than taught."

He was a fun companion, one who never tired of playing board games. He was extremely active. He didn't dress the part, but he was my faithful running companion in high school. Grandpa would often accompany me on his bicycle during my long weekend runs. I can still see him, with his polyester pants tucked into brown dress socks on the chain side of the sprocket—a rubber band wrapped just above the cuff to be safe—pedaling on a creaky old Schwinn ten-speed. He came along for moral support. He also functioned as my sag wagon. On a few occasions he'd ride ahead to purchase a candy bar for his tired grandson. I appreciated the company.

Fast-forward thirty-plus years and Grandpa was now old and close to the end of life. We were moving him into a nursing home. This formerly sharp man was now worn out. He took shallow breaths. Frail and feeble with shapeless gray sweatpants hanging loosely about his small waist, he moved slowly. As he shuffled along, he weakly clutched a crumpled brown sack with gaunt fingers. The fingers that used to snap so forcefully to get your attention.

> **I can still see him, with his polyester pants tucked into brown dress socks on the chain side of the sprocket—a rubber band wrapped just above the cuff to be safe.**

Here, on death's doorstep, that paper sack held his few remaining possessions: a few extra pair of clean underwear, a T-shirt, a toothbrush, a battered chess set, and a well-worn paperback Scrabble dictionary. In the end, Grandpa didn't need much. And what he did need fit neatly into a small paper bag. Ever the teacher, this spent old man demonstrated one last lesson for his grandson.

Speaking to logistics during the Civil War, General Richard Ewell once famously noted, "The road to glory cannot be followed with much baggage."[23] So true. We know we can't take our earthly possessions with us when we die, and yet many of us spend lifetimes stockpiling surplus we don't need. We would do well to remember that "real life is not measured by how much we own."[24]

A wise writer observed that at the end of life two things remain: our character and our relationships.[25] With that reminder, let's cultivate these two intangibles while we still have breath—as opposed to collecting stuff we leave behind.

> **A wise writer observed that at the end of life two things remain: our character and our relationships.**

CHAPTER 13
FINISHING WELL

"Anybody can race the first half, but it takes a true competitor to compete in the second half of the race."

Thirty-plus years later, I can still see the chagrin on his face as Coach barked those words at me. My not-yet-fully formed teenage brain didn't fully absorb the message at the time, but brains are like slow cookers, and those words bubbled in the back of my mind for many years. It's important to finish well. This lesson has become more apparent with the passage of time.

During my junior year of high school track I split time running varsity and JV meets. One lovely spring afternoon I was slated to run the 3200 meters at a home JV meet. Coach talked to me beforehand, emphasizing the importance of this event and the need to push myself even though the competition wasn't that stiff. He explained that a good performance could lead to a berth at the upcoming district race. He was confident I could win this midseason contest, and he communicated that goal to me.

The starter's gun went off and I established the pace. At the one-mile mark I held a substantial lead. I kept pressing but, with about 600 meters to go, fatigue set in. Confident of victory, I decided to coast the rest of the way.

Rounding the final turn, I was surprised at the amount of cheering. The loud volume was unusual for a JV meet. Swelling with pride, I adjusted my stride and began to accelerate, but still didn't go all-out. With about ten meters to go, I realized with horror the crowd wasn't cheering for me.

At that moment, I sensed another runner. Too late, I attempted to sprint.

I still have a picture of that finish. The photographer caught us both just at the end of the race. I'm frozen in time—on an urn of my own making: "Forever panting, and forever young."[26] And there is my teammate, lunging to break the tape, while my head is swiveled in his direction, a look of incredulity stamped on my face. The contest ended in a dead heat, but coach was furious with me. As a result, he awarded the win to the other runner.

After unloading his admonition about competition on me, Coach showered the proclaimed winner with encouragement. I stood by, demoralized, but also deserving of the result. I learned a great lesson that day. Always run through the tape. Finish strong.

One of my favorite Minnesota Twins players, Kirby Puckett, a star in the 1980s and '90s, demonstrated this quality. This Hall of Fame outfielder was known for running out ground balls. He put the same effort into every run down the basepath whether he produced a dribbling infield grounder or a solid outfield hit. More than once I saw him beat a throw to the bag because of his hustle. He always ran

> I learned a great lesson that day. Always run through the tape. Finish strong.

through first base. That quality set him apart. It endeared him to fans and players alike.

The importance of finishing well isn't limited to sports. A contractor I worked for during summers in college used to quote a construction corollary, saying, "The job isn't complete until you clean up your mess." He correctly observed that many of us leave our messes behind for others to clean up. He made a good point: finish what you start. I've since seen that lots of people don't do this. So many don't finish well.

The older I get, the more things seem left undone. I've started projects, activities, and books I didn't finish. I'm not alone in this dilemma. I've watched others quit mid-stride, short of the finish line. Some start coasting; they mail it in. The consequences vary, but the results can be devastating. All of us have witnessed others cave to circumstances and make poor decisions that wrecked families, careers, and reputations. Why do they do this? Why is it so hard to finish well?

Quitting is a choice—one that's often made for the wrong reasons. Granted, there can be circumstances that force our hand, but often it's our choice. When we quit, let's do so for the right reasons. Don't simply surrender. Strive to finish well. In the words of Dylan Thomas, "Do not go gentle into that good night. Rage, rage against the dying of the light."[27]

CHAPTER 14

DON'T BE AN ALPHA DOG

To be an alpha dog, or not to be an alpha dog—that is the question when running with more than one person.

In this context, the alpha dog is the one who always pushes the pace to the point where the other runners are uncomfortable. At best, this person seeks to impose his or her will on the other members of the pack. At worst, this villain enjoys showing off a superior level of fitness while exercising dominion over the group. These types can wreck an otherwise fruitful training run as they consistently push the pace to a level of obvious discomfort for the other runners.

I realize that some alpha-dogging can be done unintentionally, but in my experience, most offenders do it on purpose and seem to derive a perverse pleasure from inflicting maximum suffering on the pack. This runner has the uncanny ability to sense when the other runners are hurting, and invariably picks up the pace or throws down a hard surge—just for giggles. That's not nice.

There is nothing wrong with a good, hard run. And there is nothing wrong with running hard with others. That said, nobody likes an alpha dog. Please don't be one.

I've run with the same fellow for many years. Usually, we don't unilaterally punish one another. If we're going to run hard, then it's agreed upon at the outset. Mutual grace has been the hallmark of most runs together. But, of course, even among good friends, there are exceptions to every rule.

One perverse exception occurred many years ago on a hot and humid summer day. At the time, we were both in good shape. This memorable outing resulted in a new name for our favorite route.

The loop covers about eight miles. It circles around a lake, includes a quiet stretch along a creek, followed by a hard climb up a steep hill, and finally culminates down a gentle sloping straightaway. It constitutes the quintessential Minneapolis urban experience. We've traveled this passageway many times and in all seasons.

On this day there was no agreement that we'd hammer the course. Instead, the run started as so many do, with a nice conversation as we caught up on the goings-on in our lives. About a mile in, I noticed we were continuing to accelerate. It seemed OK, so I acquiesced. About halfway through, I sensed trouble. I stopped talking to conserve energy. Two miles later, toxicity set in.

Attempting to control my breathing, I politely inquired, in monosyllabic words, whether we could slow down a bit since I didn't feel good. "Nah, we're fine," my friend retorted. I demurred. But I wasn't fine. I stumbled along for a few more moments and then grunted out a similar plea for mercy. Again, I was rebuffed.

In the hazy fog of a pain-filled brain, I concocted a workable compromise. With considerable effort, I uttered, "How about if we both say 'uncle' at the same time?" He chuckled, declined, and surged ahead. I was done. Demoralized. I slowed considerably as he effortlessly pulled away for some distance. His conscience must have pricked him, however, because he eventually relented and circled back to check on me. Acknowledging my brokenness, I pulled it together and managed to slog through the remainder of the course.

To this day, I tease my friend about the destruction he meted out on that run. I like to remind him of one of my father's favorite sayings: "A friend in need is a friend indeed." My need was significant that day. An opportunity for grace presented itself, and my friend chose to be an alpha dog. Hence the new name of our route: Double Uncle. It remains our go-to run to this day.

There is nothing wrong with running hard with others. That said, nobody likes an alpha dog. Please don't be one.

My pal is not some perfidious pariah. He was just having some fun at my expense. Perhaps it was payback for some previous offense on my part. For, as he likes to say, "Revenge is best served cold." The story does give rise to some thought, however.

Alpha dogs are not limited to the running realm. They inhabit all our spaces and places. We encounter them often. And when we do, they suck grace out of our situation.

I'm not saying you should be a pushover. We need leaders, and there is a time to be firm. But we should be sensitive to the plight of others. Very few interactions with other people are neutral. Usually, we're presented with an opportunity to impart grace or be graceless—in nearly every interpersonal exchange.

We're given a choice as to how we respond to others. And we can choose to dispense grace. Let's follow the golden rule and treat others how we'd like them to treat us.[28]

CHAPTER 15

AVOID DISTRACTIONS

We live in the age of distraction. This malady plagues all. Pesky attractions come in diverse shapes and forms. Some are bright, colorful, and immediate. Others are muted and insidious. These distractions draw attention from where it belongs.

Distractions aren't new. They've been around a long time. That said, modern life is complex. A former Navy Seal phrased it well, noting we live in "an accelerating world."[29] In a book on margin, a medical doctor expanded on this theme, observing that, "The astounding acceleration of change and the increasing complexity and intercorrelation of issues have time-warped us into a new era."[30] Our lives are indeed filled with many variables and much activity. And in midst of our busy days, distractions abound.

Regardless of form, distractions can be dangerous. This lesson was brought home during my last visit to a favorite Midwestern destination, the Black Hills. We've taken several family vacations to these delectable mountains. Adjacent to the Badlands, this range rises suddenly out of the barren South Dakota landscape. These are sacred mountains to the Lakota Sioux. The majestic area provides a welcome haven to the weary traveler.

The Black Hills offer tremendous trail running opportunities. A run from Sylvan Lake to Black Elk Peak will get your blood pumping. Formerly known as Harney Peak, and sitting at an elevation of 7,231 feet, this mount constitutes the highest point in the United States east of the Rockies. A run to the top requires a climb of about 1,100 feet over the course of a 3.4-mile trail. The views are breathtaking, and the effort will take your breath as well. I speak from experience; I've run up this peak twice, about ten years apart.

Cell coverage in the Black Hills is spotty. The last time we were there, if I wanted to catch up on work emails and voicemail, I had to drive several miles from our campground to the top of a nearby grade, where my otherwise dead phone would suddenly spring to life with sounds and messages.

When I began my most recent climb from Sylvan Lake a few summers back, I was in cellular silence. The trail was challenging but the mountain air invigorating. The views were spectacular. I managed to run (OK, jog) all the way to the top without stopping, and I thought my heart was going to burst. The last ten minutes were brutal. Finally reaching the summit, I clambered up the steep steps of the old stone tower and arrived at the lookout spot. I ceased striving, attempted to recover my breath, and took lots of pictures as I gazed in wonder at the magnificent wilderness vista.

Once sufficiently recovered, I realized, to my delight, that cell coverage existed atop this mount. I began texting and emailing friends, family, and clients. Work mingled with pleasure as multiple recipients received a picture of smiling Dave, proudly atop the peak. Selfies possess a strange attraction. Once taken, they must be shared, right? After all, if a tree falls in the forest and you don't post it on social media, did it really make any noise?

As I began my descent down the steep pitch, I continued texting and emailing—oblivious to the hazards of downhill running. A sense of urgency controlled me because my coverage was about to lapse. Sending one last ill-advised text, I stepped on a large and conspicuous rock sitting in the middle of the trail—an obstacle I would have seen if I'd kept my eyes on the downward trail like any prudent trail runner should. Alas, not me.

My foot slipped off the rock, and I tried, unsuccessfully, to catch my balance, with the result that I pitched forward launching myself headfirst down the steep decline. Executing an artless somersault, I flopped heavily onto the narrow path and skidded to a stop just off the trail. Stunned, I took quick inventory. Nothing appeared broken although I was bleeding from three different body parts. And the face of my watch was badly scratched. I laughed at my stupidity as I lay there in the dirt, my head pointed down the mountain.

I'd narrowly avoided falling off the trail. Who knows how far I would have tumbled if I hadn't skidded to a stop? Smiling at my good fortune, I snapped a few more pictures from my newfound angle, then slowly righted myself. Brushing off the dirt, I resumed my descent—far more carefully this time.

As I said, distractions can be dangerous. This is true well beyond trail running. We are wise to pay attention to the task at hand.

If nothing else, don't text while running down mountain trails.

CHAPTER 16

REST DAYS ARE IMPORTANT

There was a loud, regular attendee at the health club I used to frequent. Rowdy, boisterous, and prone to tease, he enjoyed giving other members nicknames. These names tended to be derogatory. A tad overbearing, he'd often inquire about your workout and then retort with an acerbic quip.

Once he observed my propensity for the hot tub and the fact I didn't run every day. He coined my new club moniker as "Spa Day." Initially I bristled at the label. The name connoted a pampered indulgence that didn't square with my self-perception. It also implied an attitude of work avoidance.

Later, however, as I thought more about my new alias, I accepted its accuracy. In the running world, if the shoe fits, then one might as well wear it, and I do need my rest days. The hot tub is a place of rest and relaxation for me. Stretching gently in the hot water has become a post-run ritual. I refer to the warm ablutions as going down into the "magic waters."

Rest is an overlooked element when it comes to running. Our focus tends to be on the workout as opposed to the recovery. For some reason, many runners feel guilty taking rest days.

Water often symbolizes refreshment and recovery. After all, Ponce de Leon's elusive source of youth was a fountain. Fairy tales tell of the effects of drinking magic potions or downing enchanted elixirs. An orthopedic surgeon I know regularly recommends stretching an injured body part in hot water—twice a day. I know some runners prefer ice baths, and I'm not trying to stoke the fight between ice and heat. I'll let you draw your own conclusions. As for me, the hot tub provides a needed rest.

Rest is an overlooked element when it comes to running. Our focus tends to be on the workout as opposed to the recovery. For some reason, many runners feel guilty taking rest days. Erroneous thinking suggests that one only improves through hard work. The truth is that rest is equally important. Art critic John Ruskin once noted, "There is no music during a musical rest, but the rest is part of the making of music."[31] Similarly, if we want our running to hit the right notes, we must infuse it with rest.

I first wrestled with this requirement during my high school years. Although not technically "coached" in the offseason, Coach encouraged us to run high mileage, and we were supposed to keep a running journal and submit it weekly for his review. Unfortunately, I've never been very durable when it comes to high mileage. I realize what constitutes high mileage will differ depending upon the runner. Looking back, however, a repeated pattern is evident during my high school years: namely, increased mileage, followed by increased intensity, followed by a breakdown or injury.

The cycle was broken in the fall of my senior year when I developed exercise-induced asthma. The condition ended my season prematurely. Once I stopped running, I experienced a rapid growth spurt and gained weight. In hindsight, I don't think my adolescent body was getting enough rest because of my mileage. I was overtraining. The forced pause allowed my body to recover and recuperate. Later, the asthma improved and I resumed running. But I got a nice, long break before that happened.

I seem to be a slow learner. I've flunked the rest-test many times in the intervening years. But the older I get, the more I understand the need to recover. And this recuperation requirement isn't limited to me.

We all need rest to restore and refresh our spent bodies. Yet we tend to fight this requirement. A prolific runner advises that when training, "Rest is as important a factor as intensity."[32] This four-time masters champion defines rest as an essential element for the successful mature runner, and he instructs his readers to "learn when to rest."[33] Runners, especially aging ones—ignore this instruction at their peril.

Resistance to rest is not limited to the running world. Many of us feel good when we're getting things done. We feel accomplishment when we cross things off our lengthy to-do lists. Please note, I'm not criticizing to-do lists. Rather, I am talking about the importance of timely rest. As a friend likes to remind me, "We aren't human doings—we're human beings." He's right. We don't always need to be paragons of production.

People needn't be defined by their activity level. Constant work, strain, or overload will wear one out. And failure to respect the body's need for rest can lead to chronic fatigue and injury.

We aren't infinite—but there is One who is. We see in the biblical account of creation that God rested from His work on the seventh day.[34] The Omnipotent One didn't do this out of need, but rather to model the principle of rest to a finite humanity.

Follow His example. Feel free to take regular rest days. Rest is a choice, and we can "[c]hoose to get enough rest."[35] Work it into your regular schedule. Proper rest will allow time to reflect, recover, and recuperate.

CHAPTER 17

RUN YOUR RACE

Over the years I've run a lot of races. The most difficult, by far, was the 2004 Green Bay Marathon. That was my only try at the fabled distance. And although the conditions on race day were less than ideal, I made things worse because I deviated from my plan.

I trained diligently for the spring event. My regimen spanned twenty-six weeks, which turned out to be too long. I peaked at about four months and injured my hamstring when I pushed too hard on a 20-miler. As a result, I limped through the last few weeks of preparation.

Race day in Titletown, USA was miserable. It was about 40 degrees, windy, and raining hard. Huddled together at the starting line, my running buddy and I tried to stay warm—to no avail. A flash of lightning led to a half hour delay at the start, which only further dampened our mood and bodies. By the time the starter's gun went off, we were soaking wet and frozen.

We didn't process our pace rationally. Instead, we panicked and threw down a fast second mile —very stupid.

The first mile was slow because we were stuck in a crowd. Given our initial position, it took a while to cross the starting line. When we finally reached the first mile marker, we were horrified at the time. Had we thought it over, we'd have realized the chips on our shoes wouldn't count the interval before the starting line. But we didn't process our pace rationally. Instead, we panicked and threw down a fast second mile—very stupid.

Common sense eventually prevailed, and we slowed considerably as we slogged through the rain. Or, to put it more aptly, we kept splashing on. To this day, it remains the only road race in which I've repeatedly run through standing water. Some of the puddles reminded me of steeplechase water barriers. It was a soggy day.

Although we regained our composure and slowed down a few miles into the race, the damage was already done. My friend peeled off at about mile six, as he was racing the half marathon and the course diverged at that point. I joined up with another group of runners and let them pull me along for several miles. Another unwise move. I ended up setting a personal record for the half marathon at the midway mark—yet another poor idea when running your first marathon.

I found myself in trouble at about mile 17. Three miles later, the wheels fell off.

The last six miles were miserable. A literal cramp-fest. I was forced to stop on multiple occasions to pry loose cramping muscles by putting a foot up on the traffic barrier adjacent to the road and slowly stretching my legs.

The last six miles were miserable. A literal cramp-fest. I was forced to stop on multiple occasions to pry loose cramping muscles by putting a foot up on the traffic barrier adjacent to the road and slowly stretching my legs. I would then begin to run again, gradually increasing my pace until the cramps returned, then repeat the process of uncramping and beginning to run again. I've never hurt so badly in my life. It was a struggle.

As I stumbled into the wind, rain still drizzling down, I prayed for strength to finish. My entreaty became a short monosyllabic mantra: "God-help-me." I willed myself through the last few miles by grunting out those three words over and over.

My second half was 15 minutes slower than the first. When I entered Packers Stadium just before the finish, I avoided eye contact with my wife, who was in the stands, because I was afraid I'd burst into tears. I managed to scuttle stiffly across the finish, sorely disappointed with the outcome.

It turned out I had qualified for the Boston Marathon. I could've been pleased with that outcome, but I'd raced poorly, and I knew it. Worse yet, it was entirely my fault. I didn't run my race. Instead, after a slower than desired start, I panicked and put down a hard surge that drained my reserves. Later, I hopped in with a pack that was faster than me. In doing so, I allowed both circumstances and other runners to dictate my race. That was unwise.

It's important to be flexible in one's approach. Plans are always subject to change, so when the big event arrives, it's wise to run your own race. If you allow external forces to dictate your pace, you may get derailed and find yourself dissatisfied with the result. Don't let that happen. Instead, run with perseverance—and stick to your plan.

CHAPTER 18

PARENTING ON THE ROAD

Cormac McCarthy won a Pulitzer for his novel *The Road*. Set in a futuristic wasteland, this compelling tale follows the journey of a father and son down a dangerous road to the coast. The dad is trying to take his boy to safety. Like all good parents, he wants a better future for his child.

The book was better than the movie. Maybe if Viggo Mortensen ("Aragorn" in the *Lord of the Rings* trilogy), wasn't cast as the father, the film would have kept pace with the novel. Perhaps then I wouldn't have kept expecting orcs and elves to appear onscreen alongside the marauding bands of cannibals who constantly harried and harassed the bedraggled duo. Regardless of form, however, this story grips the audience. It's a timeless tale of a parent shepherding a child through a perilous world.

McCarthy's protagonist strives to guide and guard his child throughout their arduous journey. The parental urge to protect and provide burns bright in this grim tale. At one dark junction, the father encourages his son, "We just have to keep going . . . we'll just take it one step at a time."[36] The hero's task is singular, but it's also universal—guiding one's offspring along a dangerous route with the hope of finding a better future.

Parents everywhere can relate. Most parents want to safeguard their progeny. Yet we can't ensconce them in Bubble Wrap for their protection. As a friend once told me, "You must prepare your kids for the road, not prepare the road for your kids." He articulated a worthy goal, one that's hard to accomplish.

Children do need our help. However, no one single style works with all of our young. We often vacillate between too much parenting or not enough. At other times we alternate between indulgence and harshness in raising our brood.[37]

We've all heard stories about helicopter parents, lawnmower parents, or the Minnesotan counterpart: snowplow parents. At best, these overbearing types stifle their kids. At worst, the remove-all-obstacles approach harms those involved, including, ultimately, the intended beneficiaries.

Instructing children in the way they should go can be a trying task. But it's worth the effort because our offspring need our attention and they benefit from instruction. Proper parenting requires careful balance. I confess I've not yet mastered this art although I've had a lot of practice through raising four kids of my own. But sometimes we do get it right, and it's gratifying when this happens.

A memorable chance to shepherd my second-born occurred during a 5K race several years back. Unlike the heroes in McCarthy's dark and dystopian world, we traveled our road on a bright spring morning just before Mother's Day. Brennan was 22. He was in good shape. It was our first race together.

We started out easily enough. Throughout the race, I encouraged and instructed him as we moved along. I even took a picture of us and sent it to my wife as we were en route. Once we settled in, I surveyed the runners and focused on a fellow in a blue shirt about 20 yards ahead. I suggested to Brennan that we work on reeling him in.

The remainder of the race was spent trying to catch the blue-shirted runner. In doing so, I explained to my son the concepts of running the tangents, topping off hills, relaxed downhill running, and I even encouraged periodic surges. We maintained a consistent pace, but we couldn't bridge the gap to the elusive runner. We made progress, but despite our efforts, the blue shirt remained just ahead of us for the last two miles.

At about the two-mile mark, Brennan confided that he didn't think he could keep our current pace. I patted him on the back and gently reminded him that he could endure five more minutes of suffering. Anyone can suffer for five minutes. It's a choice. It took a little persuading—but he kept going.

As we rounded the final corner and heard the crowd cheering at the finish line, I could feel Brennan's excitement build. His tempo increased and my boy was ready to kick. At that point, I was having a difficult time keeping up with him. I gently patted him on the back again, and, this time, encouraged him to go ahead.

> **Anyone can suffer for five minutes. It's a choice. It took a little persuading—but he kept going.**

With a few hundred yards remaining, Brennan said he didn't want to leave me, but I reminded him I'd never had a strong finish, so it was fine if he took off. He accelerated away, finishing several seconds ahead of me, and I derived great pleasure watching him sprint through the chute.

After the race, we had fun breaking down the shared experience. Brennan was excited with his effort and place. He'd also listened to my advice and followed my instruction. I was proud of him. He'd done well. As I reflected on our adventure, I was gratified that I'd played a part in successfully guiding my son down the road and through the finish.

As we soaked in the post-race spring sun, the blue-shirted runner came over to us. He casually inquired if I was a coach. "Nah, I'm just a dad," I replied. He looked surprised and said, "I figured you must be a coach because of all the advice you gave that younger runner." He went on to add, "That was awesome. I just listened to your instructions and did what you said."

That made me smile. No wonder we couldn't catch him.

CHAPTER 19

VIVE LA DIFFERENCE!

As of the publication of this book, I've been married for more than thirty years. During our years together my wife has patiently endured my lawyering and my running—and, more recently, my writing. A trained artist, her medium of choice these days is food. Friends, family, and neighbors are the fortunate recipients of Lisa's bountiful kitchen activities.

She's been reluctant to claim her recently assigned family nickname, Grandma Glue, even though the label fits.

She holds the family unit together in many ways. Reliable, patient, dependable, and consistent, she possesses an unusual dose of common sense. Never afraid to speak her mind, she's been a consistent source of truth in my life. Reminiscent of King David's fearless and faithful prophet, I call her my Nathan.[38]

I've only run with Lisa a few times. She enjoys her exercise, but she's a private person. She'd rather listen to a podcast, as opposed to a companion, while engaged in moderate aerobic activity. Running can be hard on her post-surgical back, so she prefers walking. But when she does, she's a graceful runner, demonstrating excellent form—flowing from coordination she inherited from her athletic mother.

Several years ago we ran together at a local park on a Saturday morning. It was a lovely spring day and I was surprised at the invitation to join her because she usually likes to exercise by herself. As we ran, I chatted away incessantly, as I often do on a social run. Eventually, I could tell my nonstop banter was bothering her. So I shut my mouth.

> **Boundaries are good, even in marriage. Crowding your spouse is a bad idea.**

Having lived together for more than three decades, I know her quite well. She's much more introverted than me; she likes her space. I realize the Good Book says that a married couple becomes "one flesh,"[39] but spouses don't lose their individuality. In other words, the parts that comprise the whole don't disappear.

Boundaries are good, even in marriage. Crowding your spouse is a bad idea. In many ways, marriage is like a garden. The union needs air and sunshine to grow and flourish. In my wife's case, she needs more space than I do. And she often prefers silence over sound.

It took me years to figure this out. Once I did, our marriage improved significantly. Instead of encroaching on her, I gave her more room. I respect that she's wired differently than me. Some runners, including my wife, need their space. And there is nothing wrong with that.

CHAPTER 20
THINGS CHANGE

When you ask my running buddy how his day is going, he'll usually tell you, "It's a dynamic situation." He's right. Things don't stay the same; our circumstances are always changing. Sometimes change is rapid; other times it's slow and imperceptible. Either way, change is inevitable.

Unlike the characters in a sci-fi movie, we can't go into stasis as we travel through time. Instead, we change. Lady Lettice phrased it well in Margaret George's novel on Queen Elizabeth: "Things change . . . if you are privileged to live long enough."[40]

I've run with the same fellow for almost two decades. A recurring theme in our running conversations is a lament about what we no longer can do. This repeated conversation takes many forms, but it usually rehashes how slow we have become, or how much more stiffly we move, or how much longer it takes us to recover after a run. After indulging in this periodic pointless pity party, we remind ourselves how good a run we've had, and we get back to appreciating our present ability. Things do change; that can't be avoided.

A few years back, I resumed weekly workouts on the track. My goal was to improve my mile time. I wanted to break the five-minute barrier again, in my late forties. A worthy aspiration, but easier said than done. I trained diligently, ran intervals, and did mile repeats. Finally, it was time to put the body to the test.

Like all its predecessors, that time trial hurt. Unlike earlier performances, however, each lap was several seconds slower than I anticipated. It was strange. The effort hurt as much as a faster time from yesteryear. I thought I was going faster; then, after checking my watch, I thought I *should* be going faster. Sadly, however, the watch didn't lie. (It wasn't broken, either.) I was nowhere near my goal. A few follow-up attempts yielded similar results.

> **After indulging in this periodic pointless pity party, we remind ourselves how good a run we've had, and we get back to appreciating our present ability.**

That five-minute barrier remained unbroken and will stay that way. I've accepted the new norm. Times do change.

During the time I was training to improve my mile time, I had a humorous exchange with a fellow member at my club who is a few years older than me. In his younger years he'd been an elite athlete. A former Big Ten football player, he played running back in college. He'd been a stud. During the intervening years, however, this former star had struggled to maintain his fitness due to injury, inactivity, and aging.

Our conversation occurred while I was running mile repeats on the treadmill. I'd performed this workout on a weekly basis for several months leading up to that day, and often, as I was doing so, this former football player would walk past. He'd look at me and then stare at the laboring treadmill, then he'd smile and shake his head. One day he stopped in front of my treadmill and, putting his hands together, bowed his head slightly toward me and made an admiring comment about my fitness as compared to his.

What a reversal: a one-time Division I college athlete complimenting a former fringe varsity high school runner on athletic accomplishment. Nobody would've predicted that exchange thirty years earlier—but like I said, things change. Afterward, I thanked him for the kudos and then gave credit to my good genes, which make it easier to keep going after all these years. He shook off my disclaimer, reiterated his homage, and smiled wistfully as he walked away.

We all change as we age. A financial planner I know describes the aging effect this way:

- the sixties are the "go-go" years,
- the seventies are the "slow-go" years, and
- the eighties are our "no-go" years.

Granted, we all age at different rates. You may not fit neatly into those brackets. But you'll slow down eventually—it's unavoidable. You may age more slowly than your peers, but no matter how fit you are, if you live long enough, you're going to get old, look old, act old, sound old, feel old, and you will probably even smell old. There's no way around it.

As Saint Paul put it, these perishable bodies of ours decay and disappoint us.[41] He's right. The effects of old age can be disappointing. So be a good steward and take care of yourself as best you can, but also learn to accept new circumstances as they arrive.

And when things do change, adjust your stride and keep on moving as best you can.

CHAPTER 21
EVERYONE NEEDS A COACH

My ninth-grade track season was unusual. Years before my enrollment, the district decided on a three-year high school due to a combination of student population and building size. This meant ninth graders were housed at the junior high. This contrasted with the other local high schools, most of which were four years in length.

Our freshman track team was loosely coordinated. The head coach possessed little experience, and a junior high basketball coach was assigned to the distance runners. Organization was poor and there was no training schedule. Instead, at the beginning of practice, the basketball coach would ask the runners what we felt like doing that day. The result was that we did much less than we should have.

We did minimal mileage, no intervals or speed work, and no thought was given to tapering as the season wound down. The team was small and, because participants were needed for field events, my training was further diluted as I spent time trying to learn how to triple jump and pole vault. We only had a few meets. I was coach-less and clueless. These deficits were highlighted during the handful of races in which I competed that year.

I remember racing my first 3200 meters that season. This was a new event for me. The sky was clear but the spring air chilly. Excluding my teammates, all the other runners sported jerseys emblazoned with high school logos.

There were about fifteen of us competing in that race. Once the race began, I moved toward the front.

The lead group consisted of three runners from North Central High School and me. We separated from the pack early, and each time we circled past the 100-meter mark a tall and skinny coach wearing North Central colors hollered encouragement and instruction. Each time, on cue, his runners responded with adjustments. It sounded to me like he was speaking a foreign language. I didn't understand his instructions. They were like literary allusions lost on an uneducated reader.

Just after the first mile, the red-clad coach urged his runners to surge. I had no idea what he meant. Having settled into what I thought was a nice rhythm, the sudden acceleration by the three other runners rudely jolted me. I wasn't sure what to do because I didn't think I could maintain that pace. So I let them go. Soon, however, they slowed, and I worked on reeling them back in. About the time I caught up, their coach called out again—and his runners repeated the process. Once again, they left me behind.

> **The vocal coach approached me and said, "You ran a good race, kid. You just need some coaching."**

Expending considerable effort, I eventually caught back up with the race leaders with about 400 meters go to, only to hear their coach begin screaming, "Be the kicker! Be the kicker!" Again, I had no idea what that meant, but the other three runners took off and I let them go, thinking there would be time to catch up yet again. I was able to catch two of them, but I allowed the lead runner too much of a gap. I couldn't reel him in.

Sputtering and gasping for air at the finish line, I congratulated the winner. The vocal coach approached me and said, "You ran a good race, kid. You just need some coaching."

He was right. I got beat not because the other runner had more talent; I lost because I didn't know what I was doing. Those words also proved prophetic.

The remainder of that track season generated similar outcomes. Between the lack of training and instruction, there wasn't much improvement. My preparation and execution were aimless. An experienced coach would have provided great benefit. Few competitive runners succeed without good coaching. Quality coaches provide instruction, perspective, discipline, and accountability.

I ran for a knowledgeable coach in high school, and the difference was noticeable—I learned a lot. And I improved. He was constantly teaching his team. His influence was profound, and many of his maxims come to mind decades later.

The benefit of a good coach goes well beyond the confines of a track team. Proper training and instruction are useful in any endeavor. We can all benefit from the wisdom of others. I've seen this principle play out many times in my legal practice as law firms often don't take the time to train new attorneys in the art of litigation. Quality mentors are hard to find for young lawyers.

I've witnessed the clueless cross-examination of many young and energetic lawyers. Other new attorneys aggressively pursue irrelevant issues. Early in my own career, in a moment not unlike that first 3200-meter race, an angry expert witness lambasted me at the end of a deposition. "It's remarkable, young man, but you don't know what the hell you're talking about." He was right. I didn't. Nobody taught me how to take testimony and, as a result, I flailed about aimlessly at the start of my career.

Through practice I did eventually learn how to try cases and question witnesses. But the process would've been easier and more efficient if I'd been shown how by a seasoned lawyer.

My experience is not unique. Everyone needs direction and instruction in life. Some of us are ignorant. None of us are omniscient. We tend to overlook those areas in our lives that need improvement. We also tend to get stuck in ruts. A good coach or teacher will push us, guide us, and ultimately improve us—if we are willing to listen. As a wise philosopher once noted, "Those who listen to instruction will prosper."[42]

Whether you benefitted from a good coach or mentor in your past, consider being one now. Take the time to pass your wisdom and expertise to the next generation. You don't need to do it in a professional setting; rather, you can be a volunteer, a mentor, an assistant coach, or, if nothing else, a consistent encourager. It's a great way to invest in others.

And you'll probably enjoy yourself in the process.

CHAPTER 22

IMAGINED TOUGHNESS

It's time for a confession, so please bear with me. When running alone, I've been known to fantasize. OK, a more accurate description would be that I occasionally daydream. My mind can wander, and I then find myself entertaining lofty thoughts about running fast or running far. Sometimes I'll even pretend I'm winning a race or setting a record while on a run. Other times when running, I've become enthralled with my own imagined toughness for being so gritty.

I'm not sure where the need to project hero status upon oneself comes from. It's rather juvenile, but I've done it for decades. I suspect I'm not alone. While it's not likely that every runner suffers from this malady, it's probably not unique to me. All of us occasionally entertain fantasies. And if others could discern our daydreams, then some of us would look as foolish as the football-throwing uncle in the movie *Napoleon Dynamite*.

When I visit Lalaland, I'm often rudely awakened by a casual reminder that I'm just an ordinary guy. This happened again this past winter on one of my first cold weather runs. It was about 5 degrees and windy. I psyched myself up for the outdoor excursion as I drove to the club. Once there, I donned multiple layers and headed outside into the dark, cold air. The chill fired me up. It was a short run that looped around a local high school that houses my favorite dirt track. It was brisk and

I was glad to have the wind behind me when I turned to head back to the warm club.

Toward the end of the run, I began to congratulate myself on my sturdiness. Here I was, 51 years of age, engaging the elements in hardy fashion. I could've stayed in bed an extra hour, but instead I was a Hemingway hero—not unlike the epic struggle penned in *The Old Man and The Sea*. I was getting ready to nominate myself for the "Tough Guy of the Day" Award . . . when a brief encounter burst my bubble.

I was about a mile from the school when I ran by a student, casually walking along with his hands not in his pockets. His lack of gloves was conspicuous. So was the absence of a jacket, hat, or any type of headband to protect his naked ears from the biting wind. And yet, exposure notwithstanding, he walked toward the school in unhurried fashion. Waving and smiling as I passed this intrepid young fellow, I let out a laugh. How silly of me. I wasn't tough at all.

That sighting deflated the morning's fantasies. I wasn't the rugged one. Rather, this nonchalant student possessed the true grit. He was the poster child for Minnesota winter fortitude. He was the real Santiago.

Rather, this nonchalant student possessed the true grit. He was the poster child for Minnesota winter fortitude. He was the real Santiago.

I admit that his lack of winter garb could've been dictated by teen fashion, unknown to me. Or perhaps he didn't have room in his school locker for a coat. Whatever the motive for eschewing outerwear, this kid put me in my place.

Take note: all runners eventually get humbled. It happens sooner or later. Humility assumes many guises: age, injury, weather, circumstances, or other runners. And humiliation is not limited to the running world.

Radio personality and former pro football lineman Mark Schlereth once said: "There are two kinds of people in the NFL: those who are humble, and those who are about to be." His observation is worth pondering. Pro football players are a different breed. They possess a toughness that greatly exceeds the norm. And yet, according to Schlereth, they all eventually get humbled.

In the end, no matter how great our accomplishments—real or imaginary—we end up like Ozymandias: broken, alone, forgotten, or irrelevant.[43]

What's my point? Don't fantasize? Don't pursue grittiness? No, I'm just saying we shouldn't become enamored with our accomplishments. Don't be impressed by your imagined toughness. It's OK to dream, but always remember that you put your pants on like everybody else—one leg at a time.

CHAPTER 23

YOU WON'T WIN EVERY RACE

My job involves winning and losing. As a plaintiff lawyer working under a contingent fee arrangement, I only get paid if I secure a recovery for the client. I've been a busy litigator for almost three decades, having tried more than four hundred cases. And when I try a case, I either win, lose, or the judge "splits the baby."

I'd love to tell you that I win them all, but that wouldn't be true.

If a trial lawyer claims to have won every case tried, that lawyer is either a liar or has tried three cases and got lucky. Simply put, if you try a lot of cases, you're going to lose some. It can't be avoided. And that's OK because, according to the old attorney adage, "If you aren't losing cases, then you aren't trying enough of them."

> **If a trial lawyer claims to have won every case tried, that lawyer is either a liar or has tried three cases and got lucky.**

It goes without saying, but you won't win every contest you enter. In the modern era, with so much emphasis on participation, we seem overly concerned that the losing party not get their feelings hurt. That's a mawkish mentality. In life, like lawsuits, there are winners and losers. It's important to understand this reality no matter what occupation one chooses.

I'm fortunate. My racing career quickly taught me that you can't win them all. Granted, I started strong. But the zenith of my racing occurred in the sixth grade. That year, like a lucky novice trial lawyer, I won the first three cross-country races of the season. I was beginning to think it was easy and I'd win every race I ran. Wrong. That's not how racing works. As the other runners gradually got into shape, I receded into the pack.

In the years that followed, my winning percentage dwindled as I won a smattering of events, the last being a 1600-meter junior varsity race—where I threw down a blistering 4:44. (Please don't miss the intended sarcasm; as a lawyer who reads lots of transcripts, I understand it can be hard to infer tone, but trust me, it's there.) Simply put, sixth-grade glory aside, I've always been a middle-of-the-pack runner.

The decades following high school produced a dearth of victories. I had to wait a long time. In fact, I never thought I'd score another one. But the running gods conspired to grant me another win at the tender age of 49. The race was an in-house 5K sponsored by a family member's employer. The field was limited; there were perhaps one hundred runners. My entire family was present.

Once the gun went off, I led that race from start to finish. The win felt good. My winning time wasn't spectacular, but it was gratifying to see my wife and granddaughter cheering as I crossed the finish line.

After collecting some swag at the awards ceremony, my two eldest boys and I helped clean up. As the crowd dispersed, I struck up a conversation with a company employee who had volunteered to help. She congratulated me on the victory and then confided, "Don't take this wrong. But when you came around that corner, I thought to myself, 'How awesome. He's no spring chicken!'"

I grinned and nodded in agreement.

To this day, I'm not certain whether that was a compliment or a critique. Either way, she was onto something. Winning is awesome! And it's extra fun when the older fellow finishes first. That said, life, like running, will hand you many setbacks. Learning to deal with losses in life is important. A good way to deal with these inevitable defeats is to let them teach you something. To quote the superhero Megamind, "There's a benefit to losing. You get to learn from your mistakes."[44]

CHAPTER 24
AVOID DISSIPATION

On a recent weekend run I strode past several drained beer cans on the side of the road. A few other empty liquor bottles were mixed in with the mess. Taken together, the evidence suggested a heavy bout of drinking. These empty containers took me back to my high school years. Thoughts of long-ago parties and foolish behavior wandered across the back of my mind.

The remnants also reminded me of Coach's oft-repeated advice throughout high school: "avoid dissipation." Coach preached this phrase to my team on a regular basis. He often warned us of the dangers of alcohol and other bad behavior and their deleterious effects on performance.

Coach had a poster of the great runner Steve Prefontaine prominently displayed in his office. It hung above his desk. His cramped office sat just off the locker room, and Coach would sit in his old wooden chair and listen to our silly teen prattle. I suspect that Prefontaine's perpetual presence, combined with our predictable juvenile hijinks, kept the subject of dissipation at the forefront of his mind.

An Olympian, Pre was the embodiment of bold, brash, American running. For many, he was the face of the sport. There in Coach's office, frozen in time on that poster, he was running toward the camera with an intense look on his face, sporting an overgrown 1970s mustache. He was a stud.

But in addition to being a stellar runner, Pre had a penchant for drinking beer. His dissipation did him in. He died prematurely, at the age of 24, in a single-car accident. The Eugene (Ore.) police later reported that at the time of his death, he had a blood alcohol content of .16—twice what many states consider the legal limit for intoxication.[45] Such a tragic end to an American icon.

Dissipation is defined as wasteful expenditure, intemperate living, or excessive drinking.[46] When Coach used the word, he was talking primarily about the dangers of alcohol, but his advice applied to avoidance of all types of foolish behavior.

I still shudder at the memory of a high school teammate gulping down a large, luminous, green, hairless caterpillar on a run. He did so on a dare. That writhing larva was big, and when my friend bit down, a nasty stream of viscous fluid shot out of his mouth. He stifled his gag reflex several times as his esophagus went into overdrive. Chewing aggressively, he gagged and gulped on the wriggling mass as we cheered him on. Eventually, with a loud slurp, he sucked it all down.

His consumption was a bad choice. In nature, as in fairy tales, green signifies poison. And nature's nastiness pulsed with every movement of this emerald crawler. Even the birds would've passed on this snack, heeding the warning emanating from this green beacon. Not my teammate, though. Predictably, after wolfing down the larva, he got sick. No surprise there. He assumed a shade of green, although not as brilliant a hue as the one emblazoned on his afternoon snack.

Upon being told later about the dare, Coach laughed it off. Apparently, this wasn't the sort of dissipation he was worried about. Maybe he should've been more concerned. Eating a large, green caterpillar could be much more harmful to a high school student than drinking too much beer. Perhaps Coach concluded the relative harm depends on what happened (or didn't happen) after the consumption. I'm not sure; he never told us.

The opportunity to dissipate is universal. It beckons from all corners. Dissipation also assumes many different guises. It can present as an isolated event or in the form of a bad habit. All of us have tendencies that aren't healthy. Some are downright damaging. It could be a besetting sin that we coddle or a vice we frequently enjoy. Whatever their nature, we must put off these bad acts. Failure to do so can lead to harm.

When it comes to foolish living, we can go one step further: we can be proactive. Proverbs teaches that the wise person sees trouble and avoids it.[47] Whether that means not eating large green caterpillars or not sliding behind the wheel after consuming too much alcohol, the warning is clear. Avoid places and behaviors that lead to ruin.

CHAPTER 25

RUN THE TANGENTS

Running, like math, involves problem-solving. The context is geometry. The goal is to get from point A to point B as efficiently as possible. The easiest way to do this is by running in a straight line. In the math world, we could represent this by drawing a vector. However, very few runs follow unending straightaways.

Instead, like life, most runs involve curves and other obstacles that preclude us from running as the crow flies. So if you want to be an efficient runner, you must be aware of the tangents.

We tend to think of tangents as digressions, something disconnected from the topic of conversation. For example, in the courtroom, I've seen many witnesses stray off the subject about which they are being questioned. Lawyers are known to do this as well, and we have a specific name for arguments that distract the fact-finder from the issues in dispute: red herrings. But these aren't the sort of tangents I'm talking about.

Rather, when running, economy dictates that you run the tangents. In this setting, a tangent means the shortest distance between two points. Defined precisely, a tangent to a circle is a straight line which touches the circle at only one point.[48] Thus, when

> **Choose the most direct path between the corners. Doing so will save time and energy.**

you're coming off a corner on a run and headed to another turn, don't swing wide. Instead, choose the most direct path between the corners. Doing so will save time and energy, and these are resources you can use later in the run.

This is especially true if racing a long distance like a marathon. If possible, you want to cut the corners tightly and run in a straight line to the next corner. Even in a shorter contest, inches matter; races are often won or lost by close margins.

There are times to dawdle. And there will be many runs when you aren't concerned about efficiency. But if you're in it to win it, then remember the words of Charles Spurgeon: "Straightforward makes the best runner."[49]

CHAPTER 26
RUNNING ETIQUETTE

I'm a firm believer in absolute truth. My favorite author, C. S. Lewis, navigates this subject in his weighty book *The Abolition of Man*. In this short work Lewis uses the Chinese term *Tao* to describe the doctrine of objective value, which he defines as "the belief that certain attitudes are really true, and others really false[.]"[50] He provides examples to prove his point. *Tao* notwithstanding, it's interesting how social mores and etiquette change depending on context and social construct.

For example, prolonged eye contact with a stranger in an elevator is considered rude in American culture. Conversely, when you approach an intersection on a run, you'd better make sure to obtain—and maintain—eye contact with the driver of the car stopped at the signal waiting to make a right turn. Should that driver fail to spot you in the crosswalk because of an averted gaze, you could become a hood ornament.

Intersection eye-locking is one thing, but most experienced runners will ignore the glare of irritated passerby drivers who don't want to share the road. There's simply no good reason to lock eyes with a crabby motorist who isn't likely to run you over. So when it comes to lengthy eye contact, the behavior chosen by the runner depends on the circumstances—not exactly *Tao* territory.

Moving beyond eye contact, it becomes apparent that, like many cultures, the world of running has its own etiquette.

I first learned about the different rules governing runners as a lovestruck teenager while running with the object of my affection. Tiffany was a beauty. She was also an excellent runner—fast, strong, tough. We were in the same grade and I had a crush on her for at least half of my high school years.

The attraction was one-sided. I expended much energy and affection on this unattainable lovely during my adolescent years. Alas, my efforts were wasted. She simply wasn't interested in me. To make matters worse, she eventually began dating my best friend, the same fellow who spat in my face (the story from a few chapters back). But that's a different story.

Tiffany and I did have a good friendship, however, and I took solace in that aspect of our relationship. We'd socialize and study together. Always looking for a way to spend time with her, I coaxed her into running with me on occasion in the offseason. As a result, she became the first member of the opposite sex—members of my family of origin excluded—who didn't object to my flatulence. If she and I were out on a run and one of us needed to pass gas, that was fine because, well, that's what runners do. Impromptu bathroom breaks were also acceptable if required. These were not behaviors I engaged in around attractive non-running coeds.

> I came to realize that runners have their own code. What other social assemblage condones spitting, forcefully ejecting snot from one nostril, farting, loudly announcing emergency bathroom breaks, and then taking those breaks under scant cover on the side of the road.

In the years that followed, I came to realize that runners have their own code. What other social assemblage condones spitting, forcefully ejecting snot from one nostril, farting, loudly announcing emergency bathroom breaks, and then taking those breaks under scant cover on the side of the road—all without jeopardizing your standing in the group. Some running clubs will even harbor the dreaded shirtless male middle-aged runner without any evidence of shame.

I'm prone to an easily upset stomach, so it's probably a good thing that my periodic flatulent behavior is acceptable to other runners. Otherwise, I might be an outcast. Instead, as was the case with Tiffany, some running-inspired effluvia is OK. As my running buddy likes to remind me after one of us emits a little gas: "A farting horse is a working horse." Perhaps he's right. Then again, he's from Wisconsin.

The crass behavior that can be observed on a group run may be uncouth, but it doesn't violate the *Tao*. Should you find yourself among people like this on a weekend run, try to relax. Realize that, when running, it's OK to do as runners do.

Just don't engage in this behavior in other social settings. I suspect that unless you're in a junior high locker room, group running behavior will not be well-received.

CHAPTER 27

RUNNUS INTERRUPTUS

Within these pages, I've addressed goals, running tangents, discipline, running your race, and being persistent. All are helpful tools. They are essential elements for quality running. Just ask one of the most decorated runners in US history, Meb Keflezighi, and he'll tell you the "three key things that determine your long-term success as a runner are good goals, commitment, and hard work."[51]

That said, sometimes the run is about the interruption. If you're an impatient lawyer like me, you dislike being interrupted. You were on task and something or someone thwarted you. Being interrupted can lead to frustration, irritation, and even anger. But not all interruptions are bad. Some intrusions prompt reflection and others direct our focus outward and away from self.

Exploring this theme, theologian Henri Nouwen asks, "But what if our interruptions are in fact our opportunities, if they are challenging to an inner response by which growth takes place and through which we come to the fullness of being?"[52] We need discernment and discipline to recognize and embrace these uninvited challenges.

Nature tugged hard on this inner response years ago when I was running in Florida on a warm and humid morning. The grass glistened with dew and moisture dripped off the palm fronds, like rain, as I ran along a quiet stretch of road. The sun was hard at work, rapidly burning away the morning moisture. I was running into the bright morning light when I came upon a magnificent scene.

A spider had spun a large web, affixing it between two scrub oak trees located just off my route. The strands of the web were weighted down with tiny drops of water that coalesced at each junction, and sunlight sparkled brilliantly off the intricate lines as if refracted through a prism. The bright artifice was evidence of a grand design.

Awed by the effulgent sight, I slowed briefly and stared but didn't stop. I'd set my watch (and my mind) with a certain goal at the outset, and I felt constrained to stay on pace. As I ran past the web, I considered pausing to take a picture—but I didn't. Later, when finished with my run, I returned to the scrub oaks in hopes of taking a longer look, but the web was gone. I regretted not stopping for a long look.

Although my encounter was fleeting, the memory of that web lingers. In that short exposure, the ephemeral masterpiece was etched in my mind's eye. It remains there to this day. That web taught me a lesson. On a run, as in life, windows of opportunity open unexpectedly. Some of these openings are short-lived and, once passed by, we can't go back and recapture them. I'm not saying you need to slow for every shiny object spotted on a run, but when you encounter the sublime, it's worth a pause to cultivate that inner response.

> **In that short exposure, the ephemeral masterpiece was etched in my mind's eye. It remains there to this day.**

Nature isn't the only one who interrupts our runs. Sometimes it's our fellow man. Upon occasion a run provides an opportunity to be a good neighbor. If this happens, don't miss the chance to serve, for by practicing hospitality to strangers, some have entertained angels.[53]

Years ago I was running outside on a dark February morning. It was about five degrees below zero and I was about a mile and a half from the health club when I spotted flashing hazard lights on the side of the road ahead. As I drew closer, I saw a small SUV with a flat tire. It was a busy road and the owner of the car was hunched over the back wheel, his back exposed to oncoming traffic. It was dark and he was having difficulty changing the tire.

I stopped and asked if he needed help. He grunted a grateful "yes" and handed me a flashlight. While I shined the light so he could use both hands to change the tire, my safety vest also did its job, communicating a reflective warning to the oncoming vehicles. Traffic was heavy, and a snowbank on the side of the road put us within inches of passing cars. Once he loosened the lug nuts, I helped him remove the old tire and install a new one. It took us about ten minutes to change the tire, and throughout the process I kept expecting the two of us to become speed bumps given the proximity of traffic.

When we were done, he thanked me profusely. As I turned to leave, he inquired whether I might be an angel. I assured him I wasn't. I added that, if needed, I could provide him with a long list of witnesses who could corroborate my mortality. Accepting my disclaimer, he shook my cold hand, hopped into his vehicle, and drove off.

I watched him merge into traffic and then ran back to the club, cold and stiff. But that was OK. Helping a stranded motorist that morning was more important than adhering to my planned tempo run.

Sometimes it's wise to stop your run and smell the flowers while you take in your surroundings. Other times it's more important to stop and help a stranger. After all, some interruptions are more worthwhile than your run.

CHAPTER 28
THE ART OF PASSING

For the last two decades I've endured a lengthy commute. I'm fortunate because most of the ride is freeway driving. This long drive provides ample opportunity to both pass and be passed. And I've found myself irritated on numerous occasions when I get stuck behind another car that I think is going too slowly—especially if it's in the fast lane. On the other hand, I've also experienced a few angry drivers roar by me (usually in pickup trucks), presumably because they didn't think I was going fast enough.

Like a coin, the subject of passing has two equal and opposing sides. There are two parties: the passee and the passer. The event presents two points of view and provides two different experiences. We've all been on both sides of this emotional equation. These episodes make me ponder: what is it about passing other people that can generate so much sentiment?

As a runner, I confess that the feelings that take place when passing or being passed are not limited to the world of automobiles.

Most runners will admit that the sight of another runner on the horizon stokes the competitive fire and drives us to go faster. This is the idea behind "the rabbit" at a track meet. The rabbit's presence provides motivation. And for many, pursuing, catching, and passing the rabbit produces a frisson of delight. The feat can pump you up.

Why is that? Mind you, I'm asking for a friend.

This phenomenon isn't limited to my generation—although it may be hereditary, as it also infected my eldest son, Alex. Several years back I was running with him on a bright spring day. We were traversing a trail between two small lakes when we spotted another runner ahead. Competitive juices aboil, my son pushed down on the throttle and sped off toward the hapless target. Realizing we'd have caught the runner had we maintained our original pace, I found myself exasperated as I slowly reeled in my runaway son. Maintaining increased acceleration, we soon caught and then swept by our unsuspecting rabbit.

About 20 meters later, I locked eyes with Alex—and received a tired grin in response. He was enjoying the thrill of conquest. But the effort had drained his reserves. He began to slow perceptibly while we weren't even 50 yards past our rabbit. That's a no-no in the running world. You don't speed up, pass somebody, and then slow back down. That's bad form.

I decided in that moment to teach Alex a lesson about proper passing. As my son backed off the throttle, I countered with a surge, and he matched me. Soon we were really moving. OK, I admit it: sometimes I'm a bad parent. I kept increasing the pace for another quarter-mile until my son dropped back. I kept it up for another couple hundred meters and then slowed down to wait for him.

> **That's a no-no in the running world. You don't speed up, pass somebody, and then slow back down. That's bad form.**

When he caught up, I explained that a considerate runner doesn't do that to others. It's fine to pass somebody, but don't make it so obvious. Rather, maintain a steady pace as you go by. It has to do with respect, I explained. He was too gassed to reply and nodded meekly instead. Lesson learned.

As a runner, I've been passed on many occasions. Sometimes it's no big deal, but at other times it can be discouraging, demoralizing, or disrespectful. For years, my running buddy and I took it as a personal affront if anyone dared pass us as we ran our routes around the well-traveled Minneapolis urban lakes. We didn't get passed too often, but if we did, we'd surge and hammer until we either overtook the offender or got left behind, breathless and wrecked.

With age, we've let that foolish habit go, and now we usually just shake our heads and let the other runner go by without altering stride, despite our bristling innards. Old traits are hard to shake.

I remember one demoralizing occasion when I was coming off an injury and not in very good shape. It was a short run. I was coming up the final leg toward my house when two separate runners passed me in a quarter-mile stretch. And they weren't even running together. Oh, the shame. That had never happened to me on a training run before. It was too much for my fragile psyche. I returned home sad.

Again, why is it that passing or getting passed generates an emotional response? Remember: I'm asking for a friend.

CHAPTER 29

ON SOLITUDE

In my youth, several running posters hung on the walls of my bedroom. My favorite depicted a lone runner at the base of a hill with a long road stretched in front. The scene exuded peace and solitude. I've carried that mental picture with me for decades. It matched my own experience, then and now. I've run many miles with people, but even more miles by myself.

To misquote the Bard, "All the [running] world's [not] a stage."[54] My point? Running provides a great escape into peace and quiet. A solo run is a great time for self-reflection, prayer, and deep thinking. A wise author once wrote, "Seclusion is the ingredient above many which makes for strength and steadiness of the soul."[55] Running can provide this solitude.

I'm not talking about bad alone time. This isn't going up into your head when you're morose or melancholic. Rather, I'm talking about a healthy break from the busy action of life. There is value in being alone. History is full of examples of people seeking solitude for their benefit.

Running can be a lonely endeavor. This theme inspired a short story, published in 1959, entitled "The Loneliness of the Long-Distance Runner."[56] The protagonist is a gritty

> A wise author once wrote, "Seclusion is the ingredient above many which makes for strength and steadiness of the soul." Running can provide this solitude.

young man named Smith who obtains temporary freedom from bleak circumstances by running. During his solo outings his head clears and he "get[s] to thinking the deepest and daftest of all."[57] Or, as he later admits, he "started to think on the long-distance runs[.]"[58]

A cross-country race that he chooses not to win becomes the platform by which Smith snubs authority and demonstrates "what honesty means."[59] As he runs this race, he "knew what the loneliness of the long-distance runner . . . felt like[.]"[60] And while we may not endorse purposefully losing a contest, the themes explored in this sixty-year-old plot still register with today's audience because the sport does provide solitude, escape, and a chance to think clearly.

Running is a sport you can do by yourself. You don't need anyone to help you prepare or perform the act. And the joy and suffering endured are unique to the participant. Even when you compete as a member of a team, like in cross-country or track, it's the individual performance that's measured and scored.

Perhaps it's this individual aspect that attracts so many Americans to the sport. As described by a prolific author, those of us in the modern West "have a love affair with the strong, independent, self-sufficient, self-assertive hero who accomplishes great feats against all odds, with little help from others."[61]

At some deep level, running can scratch this individualistic itch; it aligns with our childhood concept of the lone ranger. The runner constitutes the rugged Western hero imposing their will in a physical contest against nature.

CHAPTER 30

ON CROWDS

The word crowd often carries a bad connotation. For example, there's no comfort in a faceless crowd. And nobody wants to be told they're:

- playing to the crowd,
- blending in with the crowd, or
- running with the wrong crowd.

We even get our phrase "mob rule" from the Latin term *mobile vulgus*, which means fickle crowd. Crowd sentiment can change abruptly; that is one lesson from Palm Sunday.[62] But if the multitudes are rooting for you, they can be a source of solace, energy, and encouragement.

While it doesn't take a village to run a race, it sure helps if they're cheering for you when you're doing it. The encouragement of a crowd provides a boost to runners. The well-placed crowd inspires.

The experience is not unlike that of the Romantic poet "who wandered lonely as a cloud," and then happened upon "a crowd, a host of golden daffodils."[63] Tossing in "spritely dance," this silent throng inspired the poet. His spirit was buoyed. He couldn't help but be uplifted "in such jocund company."[64] The same thing happens to a runner. I've experienced this positive power many times through the decades.

A crowd-inspired surge led to a victory in my first cross-country race in middle school. My friend and I had pulled away from the pack with about 600 meters to go. We were running together as we crested a slight hill before the finish. A crowd perched atop the hill and they cheered loudly at our approach. I was exhausted, but the applause worked like a shot of adrenaline, adding extra power to my legs as I pulled away to break the tape.

Fast-forward twenty-five years: I competed in the open mile at the Crimson Invitational. For the first 1000 meters I kept up with a twenty-something stud who was setting the pace. True to form, I'd gone out too fast and wasn't strong enough to maintain contact with the lead runner. I began to slow. But as I rounded the final turn and started down the homestretch in front of the grandstand, a loud ovation enveloped me. I've never had a good kick. But those cheers fueled my determination.

Awash in accolades, I picked up the pace, maintained my place, and my finishing time wasn't far off my best high school mark. That crowd contained a personal element—it included my children and my boss. And whether it was because I didn't want to look stupid in front of those people, or because I was genuinely encouraged, I drew strength from those cheers.

I'm not alone. As I've talked with others about their running experiences, many have commented on the power of the crowd. While discussing this book with a publisher, he recounted an experience of encouragement as he came off a lonely windswept bridge in the New York Marathon and heard the roar of the multitudes. That support provided a needed lift and propelled him along the way.

This experience isn't limited to the present age. Using running as a metaphor for faith, the author of the book of Hebrews describes a great cloud of witnesses who surround a runner.[65] The runner is exhorted to focus on the prize while completing the race with endurance and drawing encouragement from the crowd.

The positive power of a cheering crowd impacts all sports. Most sport teams prefer to play in front of a home crowd. Teams spar over whose crowd is the best. In football, the mystical power of the Twelfth Man even prompted trademark litigation between Texas A&M University and the Seattle Seahawks of the NFL. And in recent years Seahawk fans have twice set a Guinness World Record for loudest crowd noise.[66]

There can be no denying it: the energy provided by a cheering crowd can be potent. It translates to encouragement and inspiration: crowdfunding at its best.

CHAPTER 31
BE ACCURATE

This past winter I was able to run again after an extended hiatus caused by injury. One morning, after a short, brisk jaunt through ice and snow, I returned to the health club illuminated by the afterglow of my effort—and a bright safety vest. Swaddled in my winter wear, I walked past a trainer who, upon noticing my attire, inquired if I'd just gone for a run. Nodding, I pointed to my reflective device and redundantly added, "Outside." As if anyone would prance around indoors wearing three layers, a full head covering, and an OSHA-compliant iridescent vest.

Brimming with post-run enthusiasm, I told him it was nice to run again after a long injury break (true) and that it had been about a year and a half in duration (a bit of a stretch). As I walked away, my conscience smote me. I love truth. In my job, I encourage clients to tell the truth. And yet that morning I had inflated the length of my layoff.

Why? What prompted the urge to enhance my tale? Embellishment is an insidious problem. And it's not limited to me.

My running buddy and I have logged many miles over the decades. We've measured, recorded, and argued about times and distances covered. For reasons unknown to me, when we run together, I've assumed the role of scribe. I keep track of time and distance. He's capable of recording his own data, but like an old married couple, we've settled into patterns of relating to one another.

We don't argue much now because technology has improved. But a decade ago, our typical post-run conversation would start with his inquiry about time, speed, and distance, followed by my response based on the GPS data, followed by his disputation, concluding with my defense of the recordation. A strange post-run ritual. Yet it demonstrated our mutual concern for accuracy. In running, like life—times and distances do matter.

Years ago, a fellow runner competed in a 5K. He placed well in the event. When a friend later inquired about his time, he responded with the phrase "17 and change." Given the runner's age, this was an impressive showing—however, it wasn't accurate. The actual time was 17:58. If that's "17 and change," then I'm Abe Lincoln. It's not, and I'm not.

Why did the runner say that? His race result was respectable. But he apparently wanted more. Likely he did this for the same reason I exaggerated the hardship of my injury recovery—to make it a bit more impressive. This isn't good. And yet, we're all tempted to enhance our stories.

> **He apparently wanted more. Likely he did this for the same reason I exaggerated the hardship of my injury recovery—to make it a bit more impressive.**

An accomplished attorney I know likes to sarcastically point out that distances, height, and severity of injury often increase over time when repeatedly described by the injured person. The further removed the witness is from the accident, the greater the increase in measurements. Sadly, this characterization often proves true. Why do people tend to amplify their accounts?

Don't get me wrong: not all people exaggerate. Not long ago, I met with a client before her deposition. The case was complex. She'd tripped and fallen, injuring multiple body parts. She'd prepared diligently for her deposition and came to my office with lots of notes. As we concluded our session, she indicated she was ready to testify but wanted to review her notes one more time because she didn't want to "embellish the story." That was a refreshing statement. I've prepared thousands of clients for depositions, and I'd never heard a witness say that before. I wish more people were concerned with accurately presenting their narratives, myself included.

As we communicate facts, we should be accurate. Truth matters. More of us should follow the example of my client and seek to be honest. If we want to be truth-tellers, we're wise to keep the following advice in mind:

> Truth-telling begins with silence. Speak less and you will speak more truthfully. The more you say, the more likely you are to exaggerate, slander, mislead, and stretch the truth.[67]

If nothing else, when telling stories, try to remember the adage that a half-truth is a whole lie.

CHAPTER 32

THE GOVERNOR

In the days before Tesla, most gas-powered cars were fitted with governors. Also known as regulators, these devices limited the top speed an automobile could achieve. That way, nobody could go too fast or cause too much mischief behind the wheel.

This mechanical limitation wasn't in place, however, on vehicles operated by local law enforcement. I discovered this alarming fact on a late-night ride along with my brother-in-law, a former deputy sheriff in rural Iowa.

As we sped along unlit country backroads in Dickinson County, responding to a 911 call at alarming velocity, I gripped the armrest tightly and tried to sound nonchalant as I inquired as to the top-end speed of the vehicle. My steely brother-in-law assured me that we were nowhere close as we hurtled down the dark road somewhere around 120 miles per hour.

I wondered aloud if the bad guys would wait for us to arrive if we drove a little bit slower. He wasn't open to this suggestion. Instead, we continued hurriedly on our way, careening wildly around corners, limited only by the amount of fuel in the gas tank and my apparent lack of courage.

> I wondered aloud if the bad guys would wait for us to arrive if we drove a little bit slower. He wasn't open to this suggestion.

I'd love to claim my cowardice that night was an isolated incident and that it only manifested itself when chasing bad guys at breakneck speed in the dark, but that wouldn't be true. I've seen my top-end efforts curtailed by lack of courage many times in other settings.

Unlike the Police Interceptor driven by my brother-in-law, my body is equipped with a regulator, and it kicks in when the going gets tough. This internal voice has spoken to me many times while running. These discussions have assumed different forms over the years, but the format follows a familiar pattern.

Now in my middle years, this conversation typically occurs on a Thursday, which is my perceived "hard day." I might be doing mile repeats, or running a timed 5K, or running hills—engaged in some high-intensity effort to elevate my heart rate. Once my body reaches a certain point of discomfort, the governor kicks in and asks what I'm doing. As the pain increases, the inquiries persist. Soon, if I don't heed the voice, urgent suggestions follow.

The entreaties go something like this:

- "Why are you doing this?" or
- "What's the point?" or
- "This is good enough—you've worked hard enough." or
- "It doesn't matter." or
- (and this is my favorite) "Nobody will see or care if you back off a little."

In his book *Shoe Dog*, Phil Knight explains how to combat this regulator. "You must forget that internal voice screaming, begging, 'Not one more step!' And when it's not possible to forget it, you must negotiate with it."[68] This is good advice, but it's hard to follow.

In my experience, ignoring the voice causes the tone to

change from pleading to commanding. For example, "I can't take another step" eventually morphs into an imperative: "I won't take another step." I wish I could turn the voice off. And I'd like to tell you about my courageous efforts to negotiate with the regulator, but that body of work is slim.

I admire Knight's tenacious teammate, Steve Prefontaine, who, when faced with his own regulator "did what Pre always did. He dug down deep."[69] But I'm not Pre. And I don't always dig down deep. Instead, when the governor gets in my grill, I tend to back down. This is based on experience; I've negotiated with this entity on many occasions—usually without success.

Even though I negotiate for a living, my negotiations on the run tend to be one-sided. Oh well. There's always tomorrow's run.

CHAPTER 33

ON SEASONS

As the saying suggests, variety is the spice of life. This truth has been brought home by living and running in Minnesota for three decades. My home state is a land of four distinct seasons. Granted, spring and fall can be short-lived, but they are splendid when present. Residents lament their brevity.

For many years my wife and I engaged in an ongoing debate about the value of four separate seasons. She's always been a staunch advocate for seasonal variety. Not me. I tend to dislike change. In the early married years, following our move to the Midwest, I missed the west coast, especially Santa Barbara, the place I spent my college years.

If you've never been to Santa Barbara, consider a visit. This temperate oceanside California town is delightful. And a run along West Beach is as good as it gets—even in January. I've often said that four years in Santa Barbara will spoil you. If nothing else, the consistent exposure to warm weather will thin your blood.

Over the years my wife gradually won me to her way of thinking. The crux of her argument is that the contrast provided by the seasons makes one appreciate the changes more. She's right. The changing seasons function like a foil in literature. The distinctions deepen one's appreciation for the beauty of each one.

In *The Four Loves*, C. S. Lewis explored the value of variety in friendship, noting that our friends bring out different facets of our personality.[70] He concludes with the observation that no one person is large enough to draw the whole friend into activity. If you reflect on your own friendships, you'll find this to be true.

This concept applies to running in the four distinct seasons. Each type of run highlights different elements in both the runner and the experience.

Having run outdoors in Minnesota for three decades now, I've enjoyed the full spectrum of weather—from 100 degrees and humidity to 29 below zero and windy, and just about everything in between. The sensory experiences produced are quite varied.

Fall runs in Minnesota can be striking—when the air is brisk and the leaves are turning. Fall colors can be spectacular. The sunlight is cool and the shadows are long. The earth smells rich and fecund. Crickets are often noisy this time of year. Morning runs often reveal mist rising off the lakes. There's a poignancy to these runs because the stunning beauty is a precursor to the coming winter. It's a short season.

By contrast, winter runs are quiet, dark, and cold. The elements can be treacherous, but the efforts are exhilarating. The stillness of the air and the crunch of snow underfoot can be magical. But you must be mindful of the wind—it can chill you to the bone. Adequate clothing can require multiple layers, which means heavier winter laundry loads.

Spring presents a bloom of life. An early spring run, when the snow is melting and the is breeze no longer cold, provides a lift to the soul after a long, dark winter. Nothing beats the joy of the first spring run when you can wear shorts and not freeze. It's hard to beat a late spring run, when the air is fragrant and warm, the bullfrogs are croaking, and the birds are chirping. On runs like this, the hope of new life fills the air—and, in turn, your lungs. Alas, this season is also short-lived.

Hot summer runs bring more welcome changes. No longer concerned with footing or staying warm, the focus becomes achieving peak form or setting personal records. Depending on the time of day, these runs are often set against the rattling drone of singing cicada, especially in late summer. The humidity varies, but it can present a daunting challenge. Steamy summer runs are the best. Sometimes you can feel the heat rising off the asphalt in waves—not unlike an open oven door. I relish the heat pulsing through my veins with each heartbeat. The hotter the better. But, at the same time, I don't perform well in heat given my tendency toward dehydration. Heat saps energy.

One of my hardest hot runs ever was at about 95 degrees and 80 percent humidity. Drenched in a profuse sweat, I felt as if someone had wrapped me in a warm wool blanket and found myself becoming chilled as the run progressed—not a good sign. I've experienced the chills on several hot runs over the years. The repeated overheating suggests I perform better in colder weather.

> **From what I've tasted of the elements, all four seasons spice up the run. And the end of each season provides closure, along with a sense of anticipation at the advent of a new chapter.**

To quote Robert Frost in "Fire and Ice," when it comes to a run, "both hot and cold suffice." This is true, but when it comes to weather, every runner has their preference. I won't resolve the debate; the choice is up to you. But from what I've tasted of the elements, all four seasons spice up the run. And the end of each season provides closure, along with a sense of anticipation at the advent of a new chapter.

The distinct running seasons underscore the different chapters of life. Like a run, each season of life presents unique challenges and opportunities. Periods of darkness and solitude are followed by intervals of radiance and warmth. Often, both good and bad are mixed together. As a wise king observed long ago, "There is a time for everything, and a season for every activity under heaven."[71]

Regardless of where you find yourself, immerse yourself in the present. The season will soon pass and give way to the next. Enjoy them all, for as a semi-retired friend of mine likes to say, "Every day is gorgeous. The weather is irrelevant."

CHAPTER 34

ON BARRIERS

Henry Rono's likeness graced the wall behind my bed during my high school years. A native of Kenya, this remarkable runner set four world records in eighty-one days.[72] The poster in my room showed him in a Washington State University singlet, coming around the corner of the track in the lead, flashing his signature gap-toothed grin. He was an iconic figure, the best middle-distance runner of his day.

Another picture of Rono is etched in my mind, this one depicting him clearing a steeplechase obstacle at the British Commonwealth Games in the late '70s. This was one of the events at which he set a world record. The photo captured him in midair, high above a shimmering pool of water. As usual, he was alone in the lead.

The 3,000-meter steeplechase is a difficult race. Just shy of two miles, runners must cross twenty-eight barriers and seven water jumps—the latter obstacles consist of the standard barrier followed by a pit of water whose depth gradually rises back to level of the track.

Steeplechase barriers aren't normal hurdles that topple under you if you crash into them; rather, they're fixed roadblocks standing three feet tall. Collide with one of these bulwarks and you'll find they're immovable.

A friend of mine, who ran this distance in college, confirmed the barricades don't move. The rules allow you to navigate the barriers however you like—but you must go over them. This can be difficult. As a result, participants sometimes trip while going over them, causing them to sprawl into the water pit on the other side.

Comparative analysis demonstrates the difficulty of running the 3,000-meter steeplechase. Rono's best time at the distance without barriers was 7:32.1. Conversely, his best time with the barricades was 8:05.4.[73] Stating the obvious, the obstacles impeded him and slowed his race time.

In a shorter race, mistiming an obstacle can derail your entire race. I remember standing near the finish line of the women's 100-meter hurdles during a race in high school. My neighbor was the favorite. She exploded out of the blocks and led to the last hurdle. At 33 inches, these barriers weren't as ominous as Rono's barricades, but my friend's timing was off, and she paid for it on the final hurdle. As she went over that last obstacle before the finish line, her hind foot caught and she went down.

She hit hard, sprawling on the ground and skidding to a stop. She lay there for a moment, and I couldn't tell if she was injured or just frustrated. Tears welled in her eyes. Then I saw blood pooling on the track. Out of contention, she made a decision. She leapt up and hobbled across the finish line—in last place. Her race didn't go as planned. But she did what we all need to do when life's obstacles knock us down: get back up and keep going.

Like hurdle races at a track meet, life is also full of barriers. These challenges can come at us hard. The obstacles we face in life aren't uniform in size or frequency, and they don't stop coming. We never reach a point where we have no more troubles. And although life affords more flexibility than the track in terms of navigating roadblocks, we still must get past them as we run the race of life.

It helps to understand that life is full of obstacles. To quote a well-known psychiatrist: "Life is difficult. This is a great truth, one of the greatest truths . . . once we truly see this truth, we transcend it."[74] He's right. We often lead our lives thinking we are owed something, but we're not.

An entitlement mentality can lead to frustration as we encounter life's inevitable difficulties. We do better

These challenges can come at us hard. The obstacles we face in life aren't uniform in size or frequency, and they don't stop coming.

to understand and embrace the reality that life is hard. Josh Waitzkin, a fierce competitor in martial arts and chess, phrased it well: "The road to success is not easy or else everybody would be the greatest at what they do—we need be psychologically prepared to face the unavoidable challenges along our way[.]"[75]

The hurdles each of us face are unique. The challenges that confront us are new every morning. And the nature of these obstacles changes over time. But just like Rono and my high school neighbor, we navigate our barriers one at a time—there's no other way.

CHAPTER 35
STRATEGY AND TACTICS

I f you want to get something done, you need a plan. According to Yogi Berra, "If you don't know where you are going, you'll end up someplace else." This is true with running and life in general.

As a trial attorney I often hear about courtroom strategies and tactics—both are necessary for achieving a desired outcome. Seminars and books abound on how to develop the former and utilize the latter. Unfortunately, the terms are often confused or conflated by those who use them. A refresher might prove useful.

A strategy is a plan for achieving an objective. Tactics, in contrast, are the actions you undertake to implement the strategy.[76] The two are interrelated. To quote a phrase commonly misattributed to Sun Tzu:

> Strategy without tactics is the slowest route to victory. Tactics without strategy is the noise before defeat.[77]

This statement reminds me of some advice my running buddy's grandmother gave him when he was in high school. Following a discussion about a race he didn't win, Grandma Florence bluntly advised, "If you want to do better, all you need to do is run faster." She was right, but her advice was short on how to accomplish the strategy.

In the context of running a race, tactics are how you execute your strategy. This can include running tangents, topping off hills, surging, kicking, drafting, running even splits—or behaving like Steve Prefontaine and going out as hard as you can at the start.

Tactics are important in a race. We see this demonstrated in the preliminary heats leading to the 1,500-meter final in the Olympics. Often, the earlier qualifying races are faster than the medal round. The ultimate race doesn't always go to the swiftest runner; rather, gold is frequently awarded to the best tactician. If you doubt me, watch videos of the Olympic finals. You'll see what I mean.

My running buddy has coached for many years. He's big on tactics. Perhaps he's trying to put legs on the strategy his grandma articulated so many years ago. Whatever the reason, he's always preaching tactics. Some of his tactics are effective while others are juvenile. A few would perhaps be better labeled as tricks. Nomenclature notwithstanding, he likes to use them.

One of his favorite antics is to draw another runner into conversation during a hard run or race. A classic example involves him catching up to another runner and saying, "Let's work together." That statement is soon followed by the query, "What do you think we ought to do now?" He'll then ask short questions aimed at generating a lopsided conversation.

Over the years I've turned the tables on him with the conversation trick a few times. My running buddy doesn't like hills, and if my timing is on, I can trigger him with a political comment or some other loaded statement at the beginning of a climb. Bingo. The goal is to keep him jabbering as we run the incline. It's not very nice of me—but it works.

Talkers beware. Wasting breath on conversation during a competitive run zaps your energy. You do better to save your breath. As Solomon wisely noted long ago, "If you keep your mouth shut, you will stay out of trouble."[78]

Another favorite tactic is what my running buddy calls the "double will-kill." If performed properly, this one will demoralize the competition. We've executed this feat a few times over the years. Our best—or perhaps, most pathetic—performance occurred about ten years ago as we were running around a favorite urban lake.

We were on a moderate run, enjoying the summer warmth, when another runner sped past. My running buddy bristled; this being his usual response. Then, the other runner committed the cardinal sin of passing—after getting about 50 yards ahead of us he slowed back down to our pace. This angered us. We increased our tempo, caught up with him, and settled in behind, matching his stride. We then staggered our onslaught and my friend took the lead. Accelerating again, he blew by the runner on his left side, gently brushing against him as he went by.

I'd dropped about two feet behind my friend, but I accelerated at the same time he did and passed the offender a half-second later, but on his right. In doing so, I also slightly bumped against him as I motored past. The poor fellow was startled by the successive impacts. His body jerked back and forth from our contact and his head swiveled from side to side to see what had touched him—not unlike the reaction of Minnesota Viking linebackers of yesteryear when Detroit Lions running back Barry Sanders ricocheted through them on his way to the end zone.

After passing the offender, we dropped the hammer and sped away, chortling in our mirth. The demoralized fellow never knew what hit him. I suppose he had a hard time recovering after our double doppler effect. He didn't catch up. Amused and satisfied with ourselves, we finally eased up about a half mile down the trail and resumed our regular Saturday pace.

We've chuckled about that episode many times in the intervening years, although our spouses never think it's funny. That day, we executed the tactic to near perfection and our behavior provides insight into our puerile personalities. Yes, it was juvenile. But the double will-kill illustrates a useful lesson: properly executed tactics are effective. (Although, in our case, perhaps we were just generating noise.)

Silliness aside, the path you chart is important when seeking to accomplish a long-term strategy. This is true well beyond the realm of running. Executing a strategy requires making, and taking, tactical steps.

CHAPTER 36

TAKE WHAT THE RUN WILL GIVE YOU

There's a saying among runners: "Take what the run will give you." The idea is to avoid overdoing it when out for a run. While it sounds self-evident, the principle is often ignored. The results can be costly for the runner who flouts this wisdom.

I first recognized this paradigm in action while working as a summer counselor at a YMCA camp nestled by an idyllic lake in the Pacific Northwest. The staff would play Wiffle ball with our campers. Batters would often hit a single and then try to stretch it into a double—only to get thrown out at second base. Or they would hit a solid double and try to convert it into a triple, with the same result. It happened so regularly I came up with a slogan to warn my campers about the dangers of overreach. I called it "greed kills."

When asked how much money was enough, John Rockefeller once famously replied, "Just a little more." This principle is explored in the fairy tale about the golden goose. In that story, a farmer owns a magical bird that lays a single golden egg each morning. The farmer then takes that egg to market and sells it, producing enough income to cover the needs of his family for that day. One fateful day, after consulting with his wife, the farmer decides he'll kill the goose so he can harvest all the golden eggs at once. You know the ending: there was no gold inside that dead bird.

Overreach is not limited to summer camp or fairy tales. Having spent almost three decades as a litigator, I've seen this concept play out frequently with the cross-examination of adverse witnesses. An overly ambitious attorney will ask one too many questions, hoping to hit a home run off a hostile witness, only to get drilled with damaging answers. I've made the mistake myself; it's not a good outcome.

Through experience, I've learned a lawyer conducts an effective exam of a hostile witness—especially an expert—if one aims to pick the low-hanging fruit off the tree. Before finishing up, you can give the tree a shake and pick up the apples that fall to the ground. At that point, however, stop asking questions. The prudent attorney is content with a modest harvest from an adverse witness. If you push too hard and try to prove your case with the other side's witnesses, you'll likely fail more often than you succeed.

> **When running, it's worth realistically assessing your circumstances on any given day.**

When running, it's worth realistically assessing your circumstances on any given day. Pushing too hard or going too far on a single run may not kill and may not ruin your financial prospects, but you may experience an injury or setback because you tried to take more than was available.

Don't be greedy; be content with what the run gives you. That's enough for the day. Tomorrow may bring a golden opportunity.

CHAPTER 37
EVEN PACE

I first heard the phrase "even pace doesn't mean even effort" while attending cross-country camp after my sophomore year of high school. The camp lasted a week. A multitude of high school runners and a handful of coaches gathered at a remote lakeside location in northern Idaho. This was a coed camp—and thus a dangerous mix of hormones and youthful energy. We'd run twice a day. In between we'd swim, attend lectures, and eat. Discipline was lax and the place livened at night.

During the early part of the week we did a group run consisting of an out and back. We chose the distance, ranging from four to eight miles, and upon reaching the halfway mark our split was recorded. We then turned around and ran back to camp—with the goal of maintaining the same pace for the second half. The idea was to get a feel for consistent running.

At first blush, the challenge sounded easy, or at least not too hard. The problem was that the first half of the course sloped downhill, which meant the second half (of course) was all uphill. (Yes, this is a story about a school-related activity that really involved trudging up a hill.)

I failed the exercise miserably. Running with a group of superior athletes, I went out too quickly, running easily downhill, but then struggled on the uphill climb back to camp. I was losing steam with about a mile to go, clearly off pace, when the sag wagon drove by. That would be my coach's grocery-getter, an old faded yellow station wagon. The sight of that vehicle made me shudder for two reasons. First, it brought back memories of Coach making us run behind it while he drove twelve miles per hour for as long as we would keep up. The second reason was the driver: Coach. I knew he'd be critical of my effort.

As he pulled alongside, Coach flashed his Cheshire cat grin out the window. Looking me over, he inquired, eyebrows aflame, "How are you feeling?" "Not so good," I replied, gasping for breath. Drawing in a deep breath, he slowly exhaled and observed, "Even pace doesn't mean even effort." He then stomped on the accelerator and sped up the hill. Sputtering on his exhaust fumes, I didn't waste more breath trying to respond. Although indignant, I learned a useful life lesson on that painful run: namely, it can be quite hard to maintain an even pace.

There's a benefit to running at an even pace. Empirical evidence suggests that at longer distances the most efficient performances are produced by those who run even splits. Data derived from 1.7 million marathoners suggests that even-paced running leads to a better result as compared to going out more quickly or trying to finish faster.[79] Anecdotally, I've found that my best races involved even-paced performances. This experience evokes the famed contest between the hare and the tortoise, where a slower but steadier pace won the race.

Coach used to remind his runners that "the truest measure of athletic performance is consistency." He was right. Consistency is a great measurement in any endeavor. We respect those stalwarts who maintain an even keel as they move through the storms of life. Balanced folk are steady folk. They are reliable. Their dependability is preferred over the energetic enthusiast who, when put to the task, starts fast but soon flames out. Given that life is a marathon and not a sprint, maintaining an even pace over the long haul is a desirable trait.

Life's challenges, however, make it difficult to maintain a steady pace. Despite best efforts we never achieve perfect equilibrium. There are too many variables and unexpected changes. Sometimes a daunting challenge hampers our progress. At other times, life's drudgery wears us out and slows us down, validating the old saying that, "The problem with life is that it is so daily." This pattern has unfolded repeatedly through my legal career as I've watched excited law school graduates eventually learn that a successful law practice requires a repetitive grind. This redundancy isn't limited to lawyers. It affects us all.

> **At other times, life's drudgery wears us out and slows us down, validating the old saying that, "The problem with life is that it is so daily."**

Be aware of your pace as you stride through life. Aim to be steady. Perhaps you need to exert more effort to restore a balanced rhythm. If so, don't be afraid to expend the extra energy. Grit is good. Recognize that it takes hard work to be consistent. As you engage in this daily battle, keep in mind that when it comes to achievement, "effort counts tremendously."[80] Remember, even pace doesn't mean even effort.

CHAPTER 38

ON PAIN

My family enjoys several fall traditions, one being attendance at the Minnesota State Fair. Called the "Great Minnesota Get-Together," this weeklong extravaganza attracts more than two million attendees. People of all sizes and shapes gather to enjoy food, entertainment, carnival rides, shows, vendors, and livestock. The offerings are endless. Every year, the media previews, with relish, the novel food items that will be available. Fairgoers do love to eat—especially if the food comes on a stick.

My children claim I'm the only person they know who goes to the fair to do pull-ups. There's a Marine recruiting station. It's manned by a group of enthusiastic soldiers. A pull-up bar stands prominently at the front of their area, and if you do enough pull-ups, you win a T-shirt. These aren't just any pull-ups, however. These jarheads are serious about form. They make you go all the way up (chin over bar) and all the way down (arms locked out), and they don't let you kick. Sorry all you Crossfitters, but the Marines won't let you kip (swinging motion), either.

If you do satisfy the onerous threshold, you win an extra-large black T-shirt. No other sizes are available. The coveted garment has the Marine logo on the front and the phrase "Pain is weakness leaving the body" emblazoned on the back. I've had the good fortune to win a few T-shirts over the years. That said, I don't wear them because they're ill-fitting. I usually give them away.

In my younger years I would've endorsed this Marine motto. However, I no longer agree with the phrase. It's a one-sided and overly simple assessment of the body's nuanced messenger. Like many things in life, pain is a doubled-edged blade; it cuts two ways.

Pain is part of running. Whether it results from injury or effort, every runner will eventually encounter physical pain. When you do, be wise about how you respond. You can ignore it for a while, but as C. S. Lewis wrote, "[P]ain insists on being attended to. God whispers to us in our pleasures . . . but shouts in our pain: it is His megaphone to rouse a deaf world."[81] Ignoring pain can be foolish and sometimes lead to injury.

> **Pain is part of running. Whether it results from injury or effort, every runner will eventually encounter physical pain.**

I proved this point a few years back when closing in on my fiftieth birthday. I was in good shape and had enjoyed an extended season of running without injury. Realizing I was about to move up an age bracket in competition, I decided to work on improving my 5K time. To accomplish that goal, I ran mile repeats on my favorite dirt track, and I also ran intervals. It worked. I began to get faster. About the same time, however, I noticed a new ache in both Achilles. That ache soon progressed to genuine pain.

At first, the Achilles only hurt during high-intensity workouts. After a couple of weeks, however, they would hurt throughout my run. Eventually, they hurt all the time. The constant dull pain would be interrupted by occasional sharp sensations. I should've heeded the pain and rested. But I didn't want to interrupt my progress, so I kept running repeats and intervals—interspersed with hill work. You can predict the outcome. No, I didn't tear the Achilles outright, but I did eventually make them so sore I had to stop running altogether.

Granted, not all pain is injurious. Both good and bad pain exist. Mark Divine, a former Navy Seal, describes good pain as that which "is associated with growth and makes you stronger by expanding your resiliency and your sense of what's possible for you to handle."[82] Conversely, he defines bad pain as "the kind that hurts you physically . . . and is associated with injury and regret[.]"[83] The wise person will differentiate between the two.

There is no reason to stop running just because something hurts. With running, as in life, those who back off in the face of adversity won't make much progress. When faced with pain we need to discern the message being communicated. Is this an injurious pain? If so, heed the warning and back off. If not, stiffen your spine, accept the challenge, and seek to grow and improve.

CHAPTER 39

ON RUNNING STICKERS

There's an accomplished runner who regularly attends my health club. She's been running for decades and her achievements are impressive. She's durable and has completed many ultras. She's earned the respect of the other runners at the club. I often park by her car in the morning on my arrival.

Her vehicle is easy to spot—the backside is peppered with stickers. Some announce distances she's conquered. Others are acronyms for running clubs or events. As a proponent of the First Amendment (free speech) and the Fifth Amendment (personal property), I admit she has every right to festoon her ride with decals that say whatever she wants. That said, running stickers are a pet peeve. And conversations with others lead me to believe I'm not alone in this opinion.

The protagonist in the animated movie *Cars* had a nickname: Stickers. This speedy character needed decals to complete his front end because, like a true NASCAR race car, he lacked headlights. Fake halogens aside, unless you frequently cross a toll bridge, park in a government lot, or need to display a state park pass on your windshield, your horseless carriage likely doesn't need adhesive labels.

A 26.2-mile decal on the back of a car emits an element of brag. And when I see a 13.1-mile sticker on a bumper, I tend to roll my eyes. Why? These symbols smack of self-promotion. And I readily confess to being an incorrigible self-promoter.

My shameless social media posts prove this point—and this isn't a desirable quality. Perhaps running stickers irritate me because they strike too close to home.

The issue is self-expression commingled with pride. Many people, including myself, like to communicate. We also like to share our accomplishments with others. Running stickers are one way to accomplish that goal. That said, with running it's better to let your accomplishments speak for themselves.

Returning to the owner of the car in question, I see no evidence of pride. To the contrary, she is kind and doesn't appear cocky. Her pleasant demeanor reminds me that we can't always discern the narrative voice behind the stickers. It's said that communication consists of three components: tone, body language, and words. With stickers, we're left guessing as to the first two elements.

Further, we might incorrectly assume the narrative is autobiographical. Perhaps the decal is a leftover from a prior owner. Or maybe the sticker is aspirational—it outlines a future goal. You get the point. We needn't digress into theories of literary criticism to deconstruct running stickers, but we can agree it's hard to discern intent. After all, most of us are lousy mind readers.

Given this conundrum, we do well to avoid ambiguous self-promotion about our achievements. We do even better when we display genuine humility. A recent encounter with an elite runner on the track reinforced this truth.

I was at my favorite morning hangout doing speed work when several Kenyans showed up. (These fellows didn't arrive in a vehicle plastered with running stickers.) It turns out they were also there to do speed work. Their speed was much faster than mine. Each time the group caught up with me, I'd move to the outside lane and watch with admiration as they effortlessly sped past. Fluid and efficient, they were a joy to watch.

A little later, one of the runners slowed and separated from the others. I caught up to him and struck up a conversation. I learned they were professional runners, sponsored by a running club, who came to America for a few months each year to compete in road races for prize money. Asking questions as we circled the track, I discovered my newfound companion was in his early thirties and had left a young family behind in Kenya for the summer as he raced his way around the Midwest. He was kind and patiently answered my questions as we jogged together in the morning sun.

I pestered this pro about race times and, eventually, my lawyer-badgering paid off as he reluctantly admitted he'd run a 2:12 marathon. We exchanged further pleasantries and I ran back to my club—passing the sticker-laden car in the parking lot while doing so. Later, I looked up the Kenyan runner on Wikipedia and confirmed he's a highly accomplished athlete. He's run three sub-2:15 marathons. Yet his social media presence was negligible. Reflecting on our exchange, I was struck by his quiet humility—both in conversation and how he did his work. It was refreshing.

> **Reflecting on our exchange, I was struck by his quiet humility—both in conversation and how he did his work. It was refreshing.**

This humble Kenyan was a contrast to many Americans (like me) who plaster their accomplishments all over social media and, in some cases, their cars. We do well to remember this admonition: "Let another praise you, and not your own mouth; a stranger, and not your own lips."[84]

CHAPTER 40

ON STINK

Nobody likes being called a stinker. And most of us don't want to be a stinker. The term can be applied both literally and figuratively, as when Sam calls Gollum "Slinker and Stinker" in *The Lord of the Rings* trilogy.[85] The former label referred to his character and the latter included both character and smell. As a slimy creature who ate raw fish, Gollum stunk.[86]

In our over-sanitized modern world, most Americans don't like smelly things. We are revulsed by bad breath, rotting garbage, or Gollum's scent, the smell of old fish. As a culture we could be labeled osmophobic, a term defined as "an irrational fear of odors."[87] And since we really don't like body odor, the word bromidrosiphobia (an abnormal fear of personal odors), is perhaps more fitting.[88] Phobias aside, aversion to stink cuts both ways; nobody wants to be a stench in their neighbor's nose.

You don't have to be an avid runner to understand the sport can lead to stinkiness. After all, any physical exertion can lead to smelly armpits or unpleasant body odor. Over the years, I've run with many different individuals. Some sweat profusely. Others don't sweat at all. Along those same lines, some people smell strongly after a run while others don't stink at all.

I apparently fall somewhere in between on the odor spectrum. My wife, who's graciously done my laundry for many years, claims I emit "a particular brand" of smell after a run—one she doesn't like. She'd prefer I doff my garb quickly after a run as opposed to wandering about the house emitting my post-run scent like the Looney Tunes skunk Pepe Le Pew. Better still, she'd prefer I shed and bag the offending garments at the health club before heading home. Regardless of which option I choose, she's a good sport.

Getting stinky is a price many runners pay to run. But that's OK because, as the old saying goes, "You can't make an omelet without breaking a few eggs." For most of us, the issue of body odor appears to be one of post-run hygiene. We may smell badly afterward, but we aren't uncouth. We can remedy our malady; it's as easy as taking a shower and changing our clothes. Presto. We no longer stink. Unfortunately, however, that's not true for all.

There was a runner on my high school teams who smelled awful. He stunk 24/7. The range of stink went from bad to horrid. It depended on the hour of day and time elapsed from his last shower. The stench emitted from my teammate could've been the inspiration behind George R. R. Martin's hapless character "Reek." It was odious.

I ran with this teammate for three years. One never wanted to be downwind on a run because the smell was putrid. Morning runs were the worst because these were laid-back affairs and the team stayed in a pack. Still half asleep, nobody wanted to get close to this rancid runner. His presence acted like a jolt of smelling salts—it woke you up.

Not unexpectedly, this malodorous man was the butt of endless jokes. It was funny—sort of. But we also couldn't comprehend how anyone could consistently smell that badly. Showers ameliorated his aroma, but he still had an overpowering odor emanating from his body throughout the day. You could always tell if he was walking down a hallway in front of you. It was as if Pig-Pen had leapt off the TV screen and landed in our midst, his dust cloud replaced with a dark effluvium.

Looking back, I wonder if he suffered from an undiagnosed medical problem. Trimethylaminuria is a condition that results in an "offensive fishy body odor or breath."[89] I'm speculating as to etiology, but this fellow stunk and we all noticed.

Strangely enough, this noisome teammate seemed unaware of the extent of his stench. It could be his denial arose from embarrassment, or it could be he was truly oblivious. His ignorance of his own smell was not unique. Why is it we're often inured to our own stench even though it's readily apparent to others?

Moving beyond the scope of body odor, we see this principle at work in other areas of our lives. We're all flawed creatures. Why is it that we're often blind to our own faults when they're so evident to those around us?

> We see this principle at work in other areas of our lives. We're all flawed creatures. Why is it that we're often blind to our own faults?

To compound the problem, while slow to recognize our shortcomings, we're quick to notice the foibles of others. As was the case with my teammate's stench, we're hard-pressed to overlook the failings of our fellows. Jesus framed it well when he asked:

> Why worry about a speck in a friend's eye when you have a log in your own? . . . First get rid of the log from your own eye; then perhaps you will see well enough to deal with the speck in your friend's eye.[90]

Sometimes our flaws are evident—an overpowering body odor—while at other times our blemishes are more carefully hidden. However, we're all broken people. We need to extend and receive grace. As we run the race of life, let's not be stinkers. Instead, may we be wise to our own shortcomings and tolerant of the failings of those around us—regardless of the smell.

CHAPTER 41

DIET MATTERS—OR, LISTEN TO YOUR DAD

Ask a nutritionist: when it comes to exercise, diet matters. We're all familiar with the old saying, "You are what you eat." Although hyperbolic, we get the point. My youngest son, who is a bodybuilder, likes to quote a corollary: "Abs are made in the kitchen." He's right. And that's one reason I don't have his six-pack. What we eat matters as much as when we eat it.

I first learned this lesson when I was about 10 and training with my father to run a race. I was excited to compete in a race but failed to embrace the training because running didn't mesh well with my after-school routine—which always included a snack. When I got home in the afternoon, I liked to eat something before I started any activities. After all, a growing boy has to eat. My usual sustenance was a bowl of cereal, or, if I got lucky, Mom would let me have some ice cream. She was generous with treats.

My after-school snack routine provided a reliable rhythm for the day—unless I was scheduled to run with Dad. Like most 10-year-olds, I wasn't good at long-term planning. The immediate hunger pangs in my belly required quelling—without much thought for what came next.

What often came next during that season, however, was a run with my dad in the afternoon. Looking back, I feel sorry for my old man. He endured many episodes where I lagged behind him complaining bitterly about a side ache. I often cried as well. On those occasions he'd eventually tire of my fussing. Once he'd heard enough complaining, he'd turn back toward me and suggest, in animated tones, that I quit and go home.

But I wouldn't quit, preferring to suffer along loudly in his wake. We'd have a few more interactions over the course of these early training sessions, with my father becoming increasingly frustrated. This made for a pathetic spectacle as I followed about 20 yards behind my irritated elder—my ugly-cry face in full view of oncoming traffic as we completed our route. The passing motorists who witnessed these exchanges, along with my tear-stained visage, likely had questions about my dad's parenting style.

More than once, as he saw me go for a pre-run snack, my father would wisely advise that delayed gratification was important when pursuing a goal. I eventually caught on and learned it was best to not eat for a few hours before a run. And I finally learned that ice cream should be avoided altogether in the twenty-four hours before a run. (However, I won't digress into those stories.)

You'd think that after receiving wise counsel from my elder about food intake, I would have learned to listen. But as you've probably gathered by now, I'm a slow learner. Besides, his advice had to do with pre-run consumption. Thus far, in his fatherly coaching role, he'd said nothing about post-run diet choices. In the lawyer world, we call this a narrow reading of established precedent.

My delayed learning curve was further exposed when Dad and I ran the Cherry Pickers' Trot in Greenbluff, Washington. The 5-mile race was held at the height of cherry-picking season.

A bonus was that participants got to eat as many cherries as they wanted. I was about 12 at the time, and showing what I believed was remarkable restraint, I avoided eating any fruit before the start. However, once the run was over, I was hungry—really hungry. And free cherries were available.

Gorging myself on cherries, like Wilbur the pig, I "ate heartily."[91] And just like that radiant juvenile, I gave little thought to future harm. Alarmed at the volume of my intake, my father warned me a few times about the danger of eating too many, but I ignored his advice and gave myself to satisfying my appetite.

Spitting stones and stems as I wolfed down ripe cherries, I should've stopped to think about the twenty-five-minute drive home. Unfortunately, I didn't. My 12-year-old mind couldn't get past first-level thinking when it came to free food, proving the claim of another lawyer-turned-writer that, for some, "If you have food in your jaws you've solved all questions for the time being."[92] Thankfully my parents were gracious chaperones, but it was still a long ride home.

You'd think that after the cherry disaster I would've finally learned my lesson about the dangers of an ill-planned running diet. But no. There have been additional offenses over the years. Another notable violation occurred a few years back when I took my secondborn and his friend to dinner at Buffalo Wild Wings on a Friday night. Despite having a 7 AM group run scheduled the next day, I decided to tackle the "Blazin' Wing Challenge" that evening. That's where the restaurant serves up a dozen traditional chicken wings slathered in their hottest sauce, which the participant must consume in six minutes. Victory results in a free meal and a T-shirt.

The result for my labor? Another extra-large, ill-fitting, black T-shirt that I never wear. What is it with runners collecting shirts they never wear?

The good news: I conquered the challenge. All twelve wings were consumed in under six minutes, resulting in a burning mouth, dripping fingers, and a sauce-smeared face. The result for my labor? Another extra-large, ill-fitting, black T-shirt that I never wear. What is it with runners collecting shirts they never wear?

The bad news: I also ran with friends the next morning. That was an adventurous outing—even with getting up very early to take care of business in advance. That morning I learned the Blazin' sauce from Buffalo Wild Wings sometimes hurts more coming out than going in! And although I didn't inquire of my dad on the wisdom of this pre-run meal, I know what he would've told me.

> **Although I didn't inquire of my dad on the wisdom of this pre-run meal, I know what he would've told me.**

My point? Don't be like me. Regardless of your age, if your father is involved in your life, listen to his advice. He likely wants good things for you. And he may be able to guide you away from poor choices, dietary or otherwise.

Oh yeah, one more thing: go easy on the hot sauce the night before a long run, or you may endure more run(s) than intended.

CHAPTER 42

RUNNING INSPIRES

Running inspires—literally. There's something about the movement that stirs the creative juices. I witnessed this in a friend who developed into an accomplished photographer in his middle years. He's since traveled the world and his photos are breathtaking. The genesis of his photographic eye was a run along the Mississippi River Valley in the fall of 2012.

He's lived by the mighty river for many years. He'd driven along the road next to the running trail hundreds of times. But on that autumn day as he ran a trail by the Mississippi, he was struck by the contrast and textures of the peak fall colors. That outing fanned a desire to capture the beauty and share it with others. He'll tell you that a color-filled fall run uncorked his camera creativity. He's not alone in his experience.

Running inspires me as well. Granted, not every run, but the sport is a consistent source of inspiration. Unlike my photographer friend, I'm not an artist. My job involves proving facts in a courtroom. In that regard, I'm a problem-solver. Many times I've found myself stymied as to how to present an issue on a case, only to have the mental block lift while on a run. Analogies, opening statements, and arguments often click into place on peaceful morning runs as the physical activity jars them loose from my recalcitrant mind.

A few years back I was preparing to speak at a convention for attorneys. The topic was a lawyering book I'd written. A fifteen-minute slot was assigned for the overview. I knew the material but wasn't sure how to condense it. Sitting and looking at the material for the better part of a day, I made no progress. Finally, out of frustration, I went for a run and, as my feet pounded the pavement, thoughts soon clarified and gelled. Once done with the run, and yet before showering, I quickly wrote an outline. Bingo: I had what I needed.

I don't pretend to be an expert on the creative process. And I suspect everybody's process works differently. In college I learned that William Wordsworth often composed poetry on long country walks; the cadence of his feet helped establish the rhythm of his meter. The process caused a "spontaneous overflow of powerful feelings" which derived from "emotion recollected in tranquility."[93] Steve Jobs, the creative genius behind Apple, was known for his love of long walks. Ambulation was "his preferred way to have a serious conversation."[94] Sometimes he even walked barefoot.[95] Walking stoked his creative fire.

In college I learned that William Wordsworth often composed poetry on long country walks; the cadence of his feet helped establish the rhythm of his meter.

For whatever reason, walking doesn't do it for me; instead, my muse is loosed on a run. I find that a previously jumbled mix of ideas or half-formed thoughts often coalesce into a well-formed concept while on a moderate run. Those thoughts may percolate slowly to the surface of my mind, like air bubbles, that brew, stew, and finally release from deep within a bog. Other times I'm hit with an epiphany, and a developed idea springs to mind, not unlike the Goddess Athena, who sprung, fully formed, out of the head of her father, Zeus.

There are different theories on why this creative process occurs. My running buddy thinks it has to do with expanded blood flow and increased oxygenation to the brain. He also believes that the endorphins released during a run encourage the creative process.

It could be the physical pounding of the activity eventually breaks loose our half-submerged ideas—not unlike a piece of plaque that breaks loose from an artery wall and enters circulation. Or perhaps the steady motions on a run serve like the rhythmic contractions of labor and propel a newly formed thought out of its birth canal.

Our brains are repositories of information—Crock-pots, if you will. The subconscious works on bits of information, but it takes time for the juices to flow. A peaceful run provides the perfect setting. Deeply stored thoughts that were simmering below can release into the conscious mind, not unlike a fall turnover in a Minnesota lake, when the water temperature hits a certain level. This fall turnover is necessary to sustain the life cycle. It transfers oxygen and nutrients from deep below to the surface, and this in turn provides life to the inhabitants of the higher-up aquatic climes.[96]

Finally, there is the obvious reason running can inspire: a long run removes distractions and clears the mind. For me, it's one of the few times during the day when I'm not at someone's beck and call. I'm not checking emails, texts, or social media. The peace of mind provided by running allows for clear thinking.

I've found that long, slow, distance runs produce the most fruit. As I've written this book, ideas have sprouted from some deep well within, perhaps reminiscent of William Faulkner's stream of consciousness flow, and entire chapters have clarified on long runs, forcing me to take hurried notes in scribe-like fashion—leading to some of the pages you're presently perusing.

Think about it. The acronym for a long, slow, distance run is LSD. My favorite source of inspiration shares its initials with an erstwhile popular psychedelic drug. Coincidence? I think not. There was an entire genre of art inspired by this drug in the '60s and '70s; just ask a Beatles fan about "Lucy in the Sky with Diamonds."

But if you're looking for clear-minded inspiration, I suggest you skip chemicals—too much risk. Instead, try a long, slow run without distractions. You might be pleasantly surprised at what comes to mind.

CHAPTER 43

NO PLACE TO HIDE

I do love the track. There's something comforting about the familiar contour. I've circled many an oval through the course of my life. The memories are rich—victory, defeat, satisfaction, pain, joy, and embarrassment. These memories begin on an old dirt track located behind my middle school and span to the present.

In my middle years, I still derive solace from the repetition of the well-known circuit and often incorporate a few laps on an old dirt track into morning runs. I'm usually the only occupant during these visits. The place exudes peace and I get to be alone. This is an irony not lost on me because, as the saying goes, "There's no place to hide on the track."

I heard Coach utter that phrase many times in high school—usually after a poor performance by one of his athletes. He used it on me after a dismal showing my junior season in the 3200 meters at the district meet. I'd started well but faded badly. Family, friends, and teammates witnessed the debacle. Afterward, embarrassed and out of breath, I stayed on the track, hunched over and gasping. Sure enough, Coach strode over to me, put his hand on my heaving back, and reminded me: "There's no place to hide on the track."

I didn't appreciate his comment that day, as the delivery was sarcastic. But Coach was right. His phrase has stayed with me all these years—whether circling an oval or not. That's because the concept applies beyond the confines of the open track. Granted, a poor showing at a contest on the circuit isn't a moral failure. And failure doesn't always equate to fault. But as is true with a lackluster performance at a meet, our behaviors in life also come under scrutiny.

While that review may not be as immediate as the observations of spectators at a track meet, eventually all our deeds come to light. We're wise to remember that "the time is coming when everything will be revealed; all that is secret will be made public."[97]

We see this happen in the age of social media when an old, forgotten post suddenly springs to life and stains a reputation. I warned my children about this danger when they were younger. My oldest child didn't believe me until after he graduated from college. And, as a trial lawyer, I've seen social media posts used against clients in litigation. Beware: the bill for poor behavior eventually comes due.

We also see this principle at work with painful discoveries about the lives of some who have died before us. During their lifetime, these individuals appeared to possess exemplary character. Historical scrutiny later revealed their flaws and failings, sometimes to such a heightened degree that we wonder how they ever passed the smell test during their lives.

Other times, previously unknown bad deeds are exposed during a person's lifetime. We've all heard about seemingly kind people who turned out to be otherwise. Who isn't familiar with the standard post-horrific deed response from the shocked neighbor: "I never suspected anything. He seemed like such a nice guy. He seemed so normal"? Again, be warned—our sins will find us out.

I realize most of us aren't nefarious criminals. We aren't perfect either. We all make mistakes. As we make choices about behavior, we're wise to keep this operating principle in mind. If we do, we're more likely to avoid trouble.

During summers in college, I worked as a counselor at a YMCA camp. We filled kids' days with active outdoor adventures—sometimes with only one or two counselors along to chaperone. Camper safety was paramount. Often, during staff meetings, the director would encourage us to have fun with our charges, but he'd always remind us to be careful. He advised us to never do anything we couldn't comfortably explain to a jury six months down the road. A startling comment, but it served a purpose: it highlighted our accountability.

> **During our lifetime, reputations are built on observable behaviors. But we do well to remember that all our actions are eventually revealed; deeds done in darkness do come to light.**

During our lifetime, reputations are built on observable behaviors. But we do well to remember that all our actions are eventually revealed; deeds done in darkness do come to light. Our actions will be evaluated by others. If not right away, then later. Let's behave accordingly. This reminder can serve as a good constraint, for in the end we don't want to be measured and found wanting.

CHAPTER 44
ON INCLINES

I have a confession to make: I'm an inveterate hill lover. I can't help myself. I've been one for years. The passage of time hasn't dimmed my zeal for an incline. The steeper the better. When it comes to hills, I heed the call of that gallant Narnian, the unicorn Jewel, who exhorted his fellow climbers to move "Further up, and further in!"[98]

The mountaintop can be place of peace, reflection, and epiphany. For Moses, it was a place of revelation. I'd like to claim I am looking for an apogean experience every time I run up a hill, but that would be a stretch. Nothing that deep on my part. I simply enjoy the challenge of a hard climb.

My family has tolerated my hill-loving ways for years. Over the years they grew used to my common refrain: "This would be a great hill to run up." They heard this phrase whenever we drove up some newfound slope. And when the kids were younger, I began a strange tradition that could commence at the base of any hill or stairway. It usually happened while out exploring with offspring on the weekends. The contest began with my incantation, "Suddenly, a race!" This phrase would precipitate an immediate scamper up the impending incline. Soon after its inception, the kids would instigate this competition whenever the opportunity arose. Alas, the custom petered out as they aged.

A few years back, we revived the tradition. And we drew the next generation into the mix when my eldest raced me up a steep quarter-mile stretch at our favorite Wisconsin campground—each of us pushing one of his children in a stroller. It was a brutal climb. Perhaps still smarting from the lesson I'd delivered on passing, Alex crushed me on that hill.

It happened this way: we were running side by side, pushing our precious cargo, when we encountered a group of people meandering down the trail. There was no way to remain two abreast. Fearing a collision, I hesitated, and Alex surged ahead, forcing me to drop behind him.

What a strange scene we presented, racing pell-mell up that hill, pushing children who grew heavier by the step. The onlookers cheered as we labored past, wondering aloud at our effort. That incline is so steep, climbing gear might've helped. I tried to catch Alex, but failed; I couldn't do it, and he crested the summit victorious. Later my son asked if I let him win as he'd expected more from his old man. Nope. He beat me fair and square. (Remember, my running buddy likes to say that revenge is best served cold. Alex force-fed me a healthy serving that day.) I was dethroned as king of the hill.

Speaking of elevation, one of my favorite local parks is called Hyland Hills. I've run there for years with family and friends. Filled with steep hills and joint-friendly chip-covered trails, the venue lives up to its name. The rugged terrain beckons year-round because when the snow flies and the running trails close, the ski hill opens. It's exhilarating to snowboard down slopes I struggle to climb during the warmer months.

Stroller racing aside, not all my family members share my affection for hills. My youngest went running with me at Hyland several years ago. We'd just crested a short incline and, as we came around a corner and stared into the teeth of another climb, he wailed, "Not another hill! Is it all uphill out here?" At the time, I found the comment hilarious but later caught an earful from my wife who suggested that if I wanted my offspring to continue running with me, I should ease up on hilly courses. She's always possessed excellent insight. And since no kids run with me at Hyland anymore, she was in tune with the prevailing mood.

A few years back I coined the phrase "hill hunting." This activity occurs on vacations when I scout the local topography for the best available climb. A favorite Midwestern destination, Duluth, rewarded me with the discovery of a 25 percent grade between Fifth Avenue West and Fifth Street. I've run it several times while in town, much to my family's befuddlement. It's nasty steep.

My love of heights has driven my running buddy crazy for years. He's endured my hill hijinks on many occasions. This behavior includes poking him in the ribs, running circles around him, or throwing him off balance by repeatedly shoving his elbow forward—all done just before gunning for the crest. What can I say? I'm incorrigible.

> At the time, I found the comment hilarious but later caught an earful from my wife who suggested that if I wanted my offspring to continue running with me, I should ease up on hilly courses.

Sometimes, just for fun, I improvise our favorite route and make him run to the Washburn Tower, the highest elevation in Minneapolis. He hates that hillock. But he's a good sport and will tag along. My running buddy packs a little more weight on a climb than me. He claims our climbing adventures would be more evenly matched if I donned a twenty-five-pound pack and then performed my usual antics. And given our frame disparity, he's right.

My affection for hills goes back to my youth. Dad and I ran many an incline together in Spokane. He was a strong climber. I can still picture him charging up hills, red bandana tied around his forehead, head tilted slightly to one side, puffing like a blowfish. Impressed by his stamina, I'd try to emulate his dogged determination. His grit inspired me.

> **Dad and I ran many an incline together in Spokane. He was a strong climber. I can still picture him charging up hills, red bandana tied around his forehead, head tilted slightly to one side.**

In high school, I was taught to attack a hill. This requires leaning slightly into the incline, shortening the stride, and driving arms and legs forward. Actively engaging the climb helps me focus.

I was also taught to "top off the hill." The idea is that when you crest the summit, don't ease up. Instead, continue to accelerate for some distance. This will separate you from those runners still on the climb, and it may allow you to catch those who arrived at the top before you but then slowed down. Warning: doing this isn't natural.

Generally, after climbing a hill, we tend to relax. This is true of life in general—after surmounting a challenge, we often ease up and drop our guard. We're more vulnerable to risk in this relaxed posture. That's why "topping off the hill" is important, running or otherwise.

Over the years, I've noticed that life's challenges are like hills. Some present themselves as imperceptible inclines. Others appear as daunting climbs. Either way, we surmount both challenges and hills the same way: one step at a time.

There's nothing quite like a steep hill for blowing the carbon out of your clogged pipes. Lungs straining, chest heaving, legs burning, and arms tiring, inclines make you work. But unlike poor, doomed Sisyphus, we don't face an endless task. Our climbs always come to an end. There's comfort in that certainty.

CHAPTER 45

ON INJURIES

If you run long enough, you're going to get injured. It's inevitable. No runner is invincible. To borrow an old injury lawyer maxim, logging lots of miles will eventually cause you to become "bent, damaged, and depreciated." The condition may be temporary, or it may be permanent, but it *will* happen. That's because injuries and accidents are an integral part of running.

Granted, some people are more durable than others. For example, my running buddy is remarkably hardy. In his mid-fifties, he's been able to maintain high mileage for decades without much of a break in his stride. But even he experiences an occasional breakdown.

On the other hand, I seem to be unduly fragile. Over the years, like some avid hobbyist in pursuit of a varied collection, I've amassed a panoply of injuries, including plantar fasciitis, innumerable blisters, knee pain, shin splints, a stress fracture, a broken bone, a chronic hamstring ache, and more recently, a seemingly never-ending Achilles issue. The list goes on. If I was a football player, my inability to "stay on the field" would frustrate any coaching staff. I can assure you, however, that it's not from a lack of desire. If I haven't convinced you yet, I love to run—and that's part of the problem.

As a plaintiff lawyer, I've spent many hours listening to people describe their injuries. My job involves analyzing and assessing those ailments. Over the years, I've noticed some people seem to be a magnet for physical misfortune. My younger sister falls into this category. In addition to dealing with a variety of health issues, in the space of about seven years she was struck by three different drivers: one was drunk, another distracted, and the third driving a semi. Not a good streak. And none of these accidents were her fault.

Other people have a knack for injuring themselves. This can be described as shooting oneself in the foot. The phrase originated during the first World War, when those who desired to avoid service allegedly shot themselves in the lower extremity.[99] While it's easy to be critical of draft dodgers who resort to self-inflicted injuries to avoid duties, some runners also need to be aware of their self-destructive tendencies.

When discussing injuries, the word *idiopathic* comes to mind. Employed in medico-legal settings, the term is often used to deflect responsibility for an injury back onto the injured person. The word is defined as "occurring without known cause" or "self-originated."[100] Unfortunately, I'm well acquainted with self-caused maladies.

As I've said, running has resulted in broken bones for me. The first occurred as a 14-year-old who developed heel pain during the ninth-grade track season. I ignored the pain during the summer months that followed and did what any aspiring young harrier would do—I ran through it. As I increased mileage in anticipation of the approaching inaugural high school cross-country season, the pain got worse. Eventually, I'd ice my heel for twenty minutes before a run so I could get through it. I'd repeat the process after the workout. Not surprisingly, the pain got worse.

My mother noticed my limp and insisted on a visit to the doctor. It turns out I'd fractured my calcaneus. The physician, himself a marathoner, showed me the X-ray and told me he'd never seen a stress fracture that size. "No wonder you hurt," he said, and promptly placed me in a cast. That ended my season.

One would think that a stress fracture acquired from overuse at a young age would have taught me a lifelong lesson. But, as indicated, I'm a slow learner. And the process of self-injurious behavior has been repeated throughout my athletic career.

My most foolish self-inflicted injury didn't even involve running. It happened about five years ago. I was trying to increase the number of pull-ups I could perform in anticipation of my annual visit to the Marine recruiting station at the state fair. That year I was frustrated by my inability to get over a certain plateau. A trainer at my club, who was much younger than myself, suggested hanging a 45-pound plate between my legs with a weight belt and doing less repetitions. I'd done that exercise in my youth, so the advice seemed to make sense.

The only problem was I'd undergone bilateral hernia repair with installation of mesh during the intervening years.

It turns out the weight hanging between my legs acted like a medieval rack. The weights stretched my post-surgical midriff in unhealthy ways. And my mesh didn't cooperate. Despite twinges of pain, I kept at it for a few sessions. The resulting injury sidelined my running for a long time. And for a while, I was concerned the mesh had torn loose. It hadn't, but it also took a long time to mend. The dangling-weights routine was ill-advised behavior on my part. What is it about the propensity for self-inflicted pain that some of us repeatedly demonstrate?

> **The dangling-weights routine was ill-advised behavior on my part. What is it about the propensity for self-inflicted pain that some of us repeatedly demonstrate?**

A good goal with running—and life in general—is to remain as healthy as possible. Injuries hamper that outcome.

As we know, some injuries result from the acts of third parties or uncontrollable circumstances. Other injuries, however, are caused by our own pigheaded behavior. While we can't avoid the former, we should recognize and avoid injuries caused by our own volition. We're wise to take inventory of our own tendencies. That way we can avoid shooting ourselves in the foot. Remember, the goal is to keep running—not to prove how tough we are.

CHAPTER 46

FORM MATTERS

I've always been fascinated by how other people run. My running buddy gets annoyed with my narrative as we go by other runners. "Look at that efficiency," I'll say, or, "Look at that arm swing." Perhaps I should mind my own business, but how we do what we do fascinates me, running or otherwise.

When I was younger, and more full of myself, my observations of other runners often led me to ridicule them. I wasn't kind. As I've aged, however, grace has replaced disdain. I now recognize and respect the effort it takes to get out the door and start moving. Those who run are to be encouraged, not criticized.

That said, form does matter. And the best runners are the most efficient runners.

When we run, we want to be under control. Saint Paul captured this concept well when he said, "I do not run without a definite goal; I do not flail around like one beating the air."[101] Or as my running buddy likes to say, we seek economy of motion. A manufacturing school of thought, known as lean enterprise, has incorporated this concept of efficiency into production. Proponents of the theory will say, "The focus of lean thinking is always on the elimination of waste."[102] Runners should be like-minded.

The best runner on my high school team was a state champion. His stride personified economy. He wasted no motion. Coach would often point this out to the other runners, encouraging us to emulate what we observed. One year, Coach filmed our entire team, one at a time, as we ran across a field. We later analyzed our form. For emphasis, Coach placed a ruler up to each runner's head as they strode across the screen. The best runners didn't bob much. They had a smooth stride. Their energy drove their bodies forward.

On a recent visit to New Orleans, my wife and I took a walk down St. Charles Avenue. As we strolled down the boulevard in the famed Garden District, we were passed by many people who were running along the trolley tracks. One young runner caught my attention. I was struck by her form. She had the most unusual leg kick, and her body bobbed from side to side as she made her way past us. About half her energy was spent going sideways. As runners, we don't want to do this. We want to eliminate wasteful movement.

Foot strike, leg swing, cadence, spine position, how we carry our arms—all of these matter. That said, form is like a pair of running shoes. One size doesn't fit all. Just as you can't paint all surfaces with a single brush, your form will vary depending on body size, level of fitness, and intensity. And your form will also change over the course of the road depending on where you are. For example, if you're running on ice, the stride shortens and you keep your feet under your hips; otherwise you'll lose your balance. Downhill runners increase their stride, while uphill runners take shorter steps. And who hasn't resorted to the marathon shuffle during a difficult run?

> **Form is like a pair of running shoes. One size doesn't fit all. Just as you can't paint all surfaces with a single brush, your form will vary.**

When I'm finishing a hard run or a race, I have a difficult time maintaining a proper arm swing. When extreme fatigue strikes, my arms begin to feel as if someone has tied ten-pound paint cans to them. At that point, I tend to bind up. I must consciously think about maintaining good mechanics or my arms will begin to rise.

During a high intensity run, it's crucial to keep good form until the finish. Speaking about his win at the 2014 Boston Marathon, Meb Keflezighi emphasized the importance of good form.

> If it wasn't for form, I don't think I would have won. I think about my feet, where they're going to land. My hips, knees, legs, arms, neck. Where my head should be positioned. Where my chin should be going uphill, downhill.[103]

We don't need to obsess over form like Meb. But he makes a good point: it matters how we shuffle our mortal coil. Granted, some people naturally possess better form than others. But that's not the end of the inquiry. We can always refine how we run.

Two-time Olympian Kenny Moore wrote, "Running is a balance of physical ability and mental desire."[104] He's right, but it's also a technical skill, one we can improve if we're willing to put in the effort.

The intent here isn't to criticize those with poor form. My point is that it's worth thinking about how you run. Form matters. How we do what we do matters. And when we improve our efficiency, we improve our productivity, which in turn increases our enjoyment. We're also more likely to avoid injury.

CHAPTER 47

LETTER TO YOUNGER SELF

*D*ear Younger Self:
    I hesitated writing this because you'll never receive it in time. And although time travel is a recurring theme in literature and film, none of us can go back—just ask Uncle Rico. (He of *Napoleon Dynamite* fame.) It's not possible. That said, I take comfort in knowing you'll eventually understand the points set forth in this letter. I'm reminded of you in interactions with certain students, lawyers, and runners, those who are overachievers. For that reason, I decided to put these thoughts on paper.

My first observation is that you need to relax. I debated using this word because I know how you respond. You hate to be told to relax. There's a moment coming, in the middle of a two-week trial, when a senior partner will hiss that word at you through clenched teeth. He'll be right, but you'll be too angry to reflect on the admonition. I wish you would take the word to heart—you'll save yourself a lot of grief if you do.

I admire your work ethic and diligence, but every decision isn't a life-or-death choice. Intensity is a useful trait, but it must be tempered by perspective and experience. You're very hard on yourself. Life is difficult enough without the added pressure you impose upon yourself. Please stop "shoulding" on yourself. I encourage you to apply a liberal dose of grace to your life. This will benefit not only you but also those around you.

> **Please stop "shoulding" on yourself. I encourage you to apply a liberal dose of grace to your life.**

I no longer remember if Coach is the one who first said it, but somehow you embraced the phrase that it is "better to die than quit." Those words became your mantra for many years. You've muttered them countless times. While perseverance and grit are admirable qualities, there are times when you need to fold your cards and leave the table. This isn't dishonorable; rather, it often demonstrates wisdom.

Don't be like the person who is trying to learn to water ski but gets pulled over the front of the skis and won't let go. This half-submerged novice then gets pulled all around the lake laboring to get up. That's foolish. Instead, be willing to let go of the rope when there's no hope of getting your skis back under you. You can always give it another try later. Remember the first rule of digging holes: stop digging once you realize you're in a hole.

From this vantage, I can see that your life will present many opportunities, both professionally and personally. You'll get to marry, raise children, enjoy grandchildren, practice law, travel, run, eat good food, enjoy faithful companionship, and read great books. You'll even write a book. These are blessings. Take time to pause and drink deeply from the horn of plenty that has come your way. Life's bounty will soon pass.

You'll do well to remember the words of Billy Graham. When asked what surprised him most about life, he responded: "The brevity of it."[105] Indeed, life is short. Even now, as I compose these thoughts, I hear time's winged chariot hurrying after me. So appreciate what you have. Be grateful. Strive for excellence but be content with your place—you've been given a lot.

When you can, speak an encouraging word of truth to another. Try to emulate Dale Carnegie, who encouraged his readers to be "hearty in your approbation and lavish in your praise."[106] But don't be fake. Instead, take time to recognize and extol the worthwhile qualities in those around you that often go unnoticed.

And don't forget to say thank you where appropriate. Gratitude is like a garden—it requires cultivation. Otherwise, weeds tend to sprout and choke it off. Remember to trust God. Pray for yourself and others. Read your Bible. Accept instruction. Be kind. Readily admit your faults and be just as quick to forgive the failings of others.

You'll do well to remember the words of Billy Graham. When asked what surprised him most about life, he responded: "The brevity of it."

In closing, I give you a spoiler alert: you're not going to make the Olympics. But that's OK—you're going to do fine. So please, relax and enjoy the ride.

Very truly,
Your Affectionate Older Self

CHAPTER 48
ON GOALS

Several years ago I spent a few months working with a trainer at my health club. I was attempting to improve core strength after complications from hernia surgery. He was curious about my running and asked a lot of questions. At the beginning of each session, he'd ask me to state my goals. My responses frustrated him because I'd usually tell him that my main goal was to run enough so I could eat an occasional bowl of ice cream and still fit into my suit pants.

At the time, wool suit pants didn't offer much forgiveness at the belt line because they didn't stretch. Fabrics have changed since then, and now most waistbands include an element of Lycra, which provides more margin, a flexibility my middle-aged midriff appreciates. So when dressing for work these days, I feel like Jack Black in the movie *Nacho Libre*, because I get to wear stretchy pants "just for fun."[107]

My trainer didn't appreciate my stated ice-cream goal. In retrospect, I shouldn't have aggravated him. He was doing his job and I was sandbagging him. Of course, I had goals—lots of them. Personal and professional goals, long-term and short-term goals. Perhaps I didn't state those goals to the trainer because I was afraid to open the floodgates.

Goal-setting was instilled in me at an early age. My high school coach encouraged our team to set goals, write them down, visualize them, work to obtain them, and then set new ones. He'd monitor our progress during practice and even during the offseason; we were "encouraged" to keep daily running journals that we would submit to him once a week.

We were supposed to describe workouts and goals. Full of teenage musings, those weekly submissions likely made for tedious reading for Coach.

> **Runners like to set goals. On running, U.S. star Meb Keflezighi has written that "Goals form your roadmap to success."**

Runners like to set goals. On running, U.S. star Meb Keflezighi has written that "Goals form your roadmap to success."[108] But goal-setting goes beyond the world of running. It's universal. You won't find many people who don't have an outcome in mind. Few people are content to just *be*. Most of us, whether we can articulate it or not, have a destination or objective we'd like to achieve.

Who doesn't have a mental bucket list of things they'd like to do? And who ever heard of a race without a start or finish? You probably even approach each workday with a start and finish time in mind. Simply put, goals span a wide spectrum, including:

- faith,
- family,
- work,
- personal,
- fitness,
- financial, and
- diet.

Some argue against goal-setting. Scott Adams, creator of the Dilbert comic strip, is an ardent critic of goals. As he puts it, "goals are for losers."[109] He writes that goal-driven people "exist in a state of nearly continuous failure" that may wear them out. Achieving a goal only leads to temporary satisfaction, he explains, because then one must set another goal and restart the frustrating process. And those who fail to meet their goals may experience a sense of "permanent failure."[110] Adams makes valid points.

We've all likely encountered the dilemma of failing to reach an objective. A goal is set, hard work is performed, but the result falls short. I experienced this in my only attempt at a marathon. I'd set a goal. In the months that followed, I trained extremely hard, but when race time came, I fell short. I felt as if I'd failed and let myself down. My marathon experience illustrates Adams's concerns about setting goals. But even a lofty goal can be useful. Perhaps you've aimed for the stars but only landed on the moon. At least you made it into space.

> I'd set a goal. In the months that followed, I trained extremely hard, but when race time came, I fell short. I felt as if I'd failed.

Despite the frustration of failure, I think goals are useful. Having an objective in mind helps you focus and achieve an ultimate outcome. Goals allow you to chart a course or outline a path to an ultimate destination. As the old saying goes, "If you don't know where you're going, any train will get you there." Proper goals can help channel efforts.

Simply setting a goal won't help you achieve that goal, however. You've got to do the work. As a litigator, my objective is to secure a successful outcome for the client. This often involves trying a case. To successfully try a case, you must do the work, prepare, and then, when the time comes for the courtroom, you need to execute. All the hard work and preparation won't pay off in the end if you drop the ball at trial.

I've been accused of being aspirational in my vocation. This was pointed out by a certain judge when I was a younger attorney. It began with an overreach I made at a settlement conference on a weak case the first time I appeared before this judge. He called out my approach that day. And he was right: I was looking for too much. Ever after, when I saw him at court, he'd teasingly inquire if I was still looking for the world with a white picket fence around it.

It's OK to be aspirational, but one should also be realistic about goals. Setting an unattainable objective can lead to frustration. Conversely, a goal that is too easily accomplished doesn't provide any gratification and won't lead to improvement.

We also need to recognize the interplay between short-term goals and long-term goals. There's tension here. Long-term goals need to be reevaluated as circumstances change. We need balance because sometimes short-term goals override long-term goals. We must always be aware of the tyranny of the urgent. Don't let the immediate override the important.

Setting effective goals also requires accountability. After all, what's the use of setting goals and not following through? One should also be wary of setting vague goals; a good example of this is my desire to eat a bowl of ice cream. That one is hard to measure. How do you know if you achieved your goal?

Danger also exists when you become a slave to a goal. In those situations, the goal becomes a taskmaster and everything else must give way. Single-mindedness is good, but not ultimate. A goal is a means to an end, not the other way around.

In the final analysis, goals can both help and hinder. Used properly, goals are tools we use to achieve and improve whether we're talking about running or some other aspect of life. And although a goal may look like an ultimate outcome, life (like running) is about the journey. May we learn to enjoy the process as opposed to fixating on the result.

CHAPTER 49

ON TIMING

As with life in general, timing is crucial when it comes to running. My running buddy is a track coach. During the spring, he'll often talk about the importance of preparing his runners to peak at the end of the season. He plans and plots to help his runners achieve their best performance. Timing is key in this process. Sometimes it's on and other times it's not.

Lasse Viren, known as "the Flying Finn," was a master at sharpening his performance for the big stage. This Olympic champion has been described as:

> . . . a winner of very little besides four golden medals, two each at the 5,000M and 10,000M in the 1972 and 1976 Olympic Games—[he] appeared to be an "ordinary" athlete in non-Olympic years, but beat the world by . . . choosing to peak only once every four years.[111]

Timing in running has more to do than just peaking. If you've never watched the finals of the 1972 Olympic 800-meter race, I advise you to do it. You're in for a treat. In that race, American Dave Wottle made a thrilling comeback. Trailing by about 20 meters in the early part of the race, he was in eighth place (dead last) at the halfway mark. Passing two runners, he remained in sixth place with 200 meters left. The gap in front of him appeared too large to overcome.

Wottle managed to move up to fourth place with 100 meters to go, but he still trailed the lead runner by about ten meters. My dad remembers watching that race unfold on TV. He was yelling at the screen as Wottle made his move; my dad thought Wottle had waited too long. Nope. "Wottle the Throttle" mustered a blistering kick to win the gold medal by .03 seconds—an inspiring finish. And just in time.

If you've never watched the finals of the 1972 Olympic 800-meter race, I advise you to do it. You're in for a treat.

My own experience with timing falls short of Olympic stature. Somehow, I managed to peak about six weeks before my marathon. And I seem to possess a remarkable knack for injury whenever I approach an optimal level of fitness.

However, my most memorable example of bad timing on a run concluded with an unfortunate shower scene (no, not like the one in the movie *Psycho*).

True to form, I'd eaten something I shouldn't have the night before a long weekend jaunt with my running buddy. My stomach rebelled as we traveled a familiar route. Toward the end, I was in trouble. We were running through a crowded neighborhood. No bathrooms were available between our location and his house. As a result, I ran stiffly and clenched the best I could. Sensing my dilemma, he suggested I run ahead and make straight for his house. He assured me nobody was home and I could go straight to the bathroom. I accepted his word and ran as hard as my body would allow.

Tearing open the back door and sprinting through his house, I wasn't sure I was going to make it. As I burst into the bathroom, I realized—with dismay—that the shower was running. By then I was completely in the bathroom, standing in front of the shower, and in dire condition. It turns out my running buddy was wrong—his wife was home. And in the shower. Oops. Bad timing on several fronts.

My bathroom debacle reminds me of the wise words of a former professor who noted, "Everything worthwhile has its time and place, but not the same time nor place."[112] How you do what you do is important.

Equally important, however, is *when* you do it. This is true in sports, politics, relationships, and work—and when visiting the bathroom. Timing matters.

CHAPTER 50

ON GRANDPARENTING

Grandkids are a hoot. They are a tremendous source of joy. There's something surreal about holding the child of your child. As of this writing, I have three of them, one for each decade of marriage.

During a recent discussion about grandchildren, another lawyer inquired whether I see my grandkids often. I answered, "No. Just once or twice per week." The incredulous look I received in response made me pause. I'd answered thinking of my wife, who visits them several times per week. The attorney told me that she sees her grandkids twice a year. She then asked if they lived nearby and I responded, "Not too close—about twenty minutes away." I said that because the other set of grandparents lives about a quarter-mile from my grandkids. My reply generated another baffled look. It turns out this attorney's grandkids live four states away.

Having reflected on the geography, I now agree: they do live close by. In fact, if I add an extra loop in my neighborhood, it's exactly 13.1 miles to my grandchildren's house. I've run the route several times. I named it "The Hadley Half" in honor of my firstborn grandchild. It's a good fitness test because it starts out going downhill, then across the Minnesota River Valley, and finishes with about four miles of rolling hills. Those hills are hard work, but it's a gratifying run. At the end I get to visit the grandkids—a worthy goal.

When it comes to life, my dad likes to say that showing up is about 90 percent of the battle. This statement proves true as I reflect on my grandparents and their influence on my life. They were present and engaged. They would come to my track meets and cross-country races and cheer heartily, which was kind. Some track meets drew a crowd, but most cross-country races didn't. I appreciated their support. Grandpa also would often accompany me on longer runs in high school. My grandparents were a significant part of my growing up, and now that I'm a grandparent, I want to emulate their example.

Shortly before my fiftieth birthday, I took a lovely fall run. Afterward, I floated in the pool at the club to cool down. Laying half-submerged in the water, I prayed for both my grandmother (who was still alive) and my granddaughter. The two were born about one hundred years apart. What a unique position I occupied at that time—simultaneously a grandchild of a living grandparent and a grandparent myself. How cool is that? As I reflected on the blessings bestowed on me by my grandparents, I was inspired to do the same for my grandkids.

One fun way to spend time with my grandchildren is to push them in a stroller on a run. My son and I have spent many sunny weekend mornings pushing Hadley as we ran through the wooded trails around his house. Those outings have given me quality time with two generations at once.

> **What a unique position I occupied at that time—simultaneously a grandchild of a living grandparent and a grandparent myself. How cool is that?**

We've even included Hadley in our hill work. A couple of years back, after we finished our route, I suggested to Alex that we run repeats on an elevation in his neighborhood. It's a gentle slope on a quiet street—perfect for stroller-pushing risers. Alex and I ran up it several times. Hadley, giggling, thought it was fun to race repeatedly up that incline against her dad. For Alex and me, the added resistance increased the intensity of the workout. It was good family fun. Finally, a neighbor came out of her house to see what we were doing. I explained and she nodded, but the look on her face suggested the explanation didn't register.

Pushing a grandchild in a stroller can calm them when they're upset. My secondborn grandchild has special needs. This child loves the vibration created by the road, and he's often content to let you push him all over the place. This is a double bonus because it provides a break for his parents and gives me extra time with my grandson. It's a rush to push your child's child on a run. It always leaves me reflecting on my good fortune. Grandchildren are indeed "the crown of the aged."[113]

I'm not suggesting you force grandchildren to fit your schedule. Making them participate in the activities we want to do, regardless of their interest, doesn't lead to meaningful connection. Don't make them hostage to your lifestyle. Rather, my point is, for some, running provides an avenue for spending quality time with distant offspring. My grandparents engaged with me, and running has provided an opportunity for me to interact with my grandkids.

Take time to enjoy your offspring, children and grandchildren alike. Incorporate them into your activities. Spend time with them. The goal is to make memories and establish relationships. You won't regret the time you invest in the next generation. It's a great way to pay your blessings forward.

CHAPTER 51

PET THE TIGER

Coach used to say that in every race there comes a decisive moment, where in order to succeed, you must "pet the tiger." He preached this message regularly. His point was that if you want to go to the next level, there comes a time when you've got to take a chance. This involves risk. And there is often an element of fear at this juncture: can I do this? What will happen if I take this chance and fall short?

I don't know if Coach was a fan of Romantic poetry, but his phrase evokes images from a famous sonnet penned by William Blake, "The Tyger." This work explores the audacity of the creative mind that envisioned and then brought forth the fierce tiger.

> Tyger Tyger burning bright, in the forests of the night; what immortal hand or eye, could frame thy fearful symmetry?[114]

A few stanzas later, after describing the mighty beast, Blake asks a similar but slightly different question: he wonders what being would dare to create this animal. For Blake, the question is rhetorical.

Whether Coach intended the allusion when he exhorted us to "pet the tiger," Blake's fierce image illustrates the danger of the big cat. My wife and I recently visited the Phoenix Zoo and we watched the tigers pacing about at feeding time, their tales a 'twitch. The felines growled and glared as they gulped down food provided by their well-protected handlers. No petting was involved. The mealtime message was clear—there's risk when you get close to a tiger.

Petting the tiger also includes a volitional aspect. You're choosing to engage the challenge. The 1980s rock band Survivor capitalized on this theme with their enduring song, "The Eye of the Tiger." Included in the soundtrack for the movie *Rocky III*, the lyrics talk about fighting to keep your dream alive and the refrain repeatedly mentions the eye of the tiger.

> **Petting the tiger also includes a volitional aspect. You're choosing to engage the challenge.**

The song encourages risk-taking, and the tune will get your blood pumping. If you don't believe me, take a listen. It's an effective tune. Keflezighi, the champion marathoner, admits he listens to the song before a race to fire himself up.[115] One of my own high school teammates listened to the song the night before the state meet, and he later told us the refrain kept playing in his head as he ran his way to a state championship, a race in which he ran negative splits. This champion "pet the tiger"—and it paid dividends.

Sometimes "you pet the tiger" and fall short. Steve Prefontaine's 5000-meter race in the 1972 Olympics provides a good example of a risk taken that didn't pay off. The race didn't go according to plan. It started slowly. Pre took the lead about two miles in, but then relinquished it. Running in the lead group with about 300 meters to go, he probably could've waited, then kicked, and earned himself a lower spot on the podium, but he chose not to do that. Instead, he went for gold.

Twice in the last 200 meters Pre tried to pass the lead runners. Both times he got cut off. With 100 meters to go he tried to kick and "there was no response. Totally spent, he staggered the last dozen meters and was passed[.]"[116] He finished out of medal contention. He was heartbroken. But he ran the race to win it. He took a risk and came up short.

Risk is associated with any venture, running or otherwise. There comes a point when a participant assesses the danger, but sensing opportunity decides to press on. I'm not talking about foolhardy behavior, but calculated decision-making. The old saying is on point: "Nothing ventured, nothing gained."

My father-in-law was an orthodontist with a successful practice. Right about the time his kids were entering college, he made a large financial gamble. He and a partner started a motel chain in Iowa known as the Heartland Inns. To do this, he mortgaged everything he owned. He leveraged himself to the point that failure of the venture would have bankrupted him. It didn't—and he wasn't. It turned out to be a savvy move, but there were no guarantees at the outset.

That's how it is with risk-taking. As climber Alex Honnold says during the documentary *Free Solo*, "You face your fear because the goal demands it."[117] If you want to succeed, you've got to take risks. Sometimes they pay off and, at other times, they don't.

It can be hard to take risks. "Often it is easier to step down to the lower level, to easier assignments, to less responsibility, than it is to enter a larger door."[118] Success requires taking risks.

If we want to succeed, there will come moments when we must "pet the tiger."

CHAPTER 52

ON BREATHING

The number of breaths taken per minute is called a person's respiratory rate. The normal respiratory rate for an adult at rest is twelve to twenty breaths per minute.[119] Exercising intensely, this rate may elevate to forty to fifty breaths per minute.[120] But aside from that difference, our breathing is so natural that, typically, we don't think about it.

Breathing is elemental and yet so important. Attention is paid to our breathing at the beginning and end of our lives—but not so often in between. Having witnessed the births of four children, I can attest that one of the first things the doctor checks is to make sure the child is breathing on its own. And when it comes to death, the final breath is often the last activity observed.

Other than holding my breath in a swimming pool as a youngster, the first time I remember attempting to control my breathing was in junior high. I had a late lunch period and would often run right after school. This would invariably lead to a side ache. These hurt. Another runner gave me some advice on how to run through them. I was told to push my diaphragm out in an exaggerated fashion while inhaling. It took practice, but I eventually learned the technique. I'm pleased to say it helped.

In high school, I took respiratory awareness a step further when I began to listen for the breathing pattern of other runners who were close by me during a race or hard run. The harder they were breathing, the more likely they were suffering. If so, perhaps I could drop them with a hard surge. The converse was also true, so I often attempted to control ragged breathing during a contest so that those in proximity wouldn't discern how badly I was hurting. There was no need to invite further pain.

And what runner isn't familiar with the conversational run? The pace of this easy workout allows you to engage in back and forth banter without losing your breath. These talkative times comprise my favorite outings with my running buddy. But I've endured many workouts where running and talking couldn't coexist.

One embarrassing episode happened during a recent visit to Waco, Texas to see my youngest child, who was attending Baylor University.

I went on a morning run and, upon approaching the rugby practice field, realized my route was going to intersect with that of a younger runner. He was going faster than me, but I sped up, joined him, and we talked for about a mile. I learned a lot about this recent graduate who was planning to enroll in medical school. We were moving at a fast clip, and our chatter quickly drained my running reserves. Soon it was hard to maintain the conversation and my breathing became ragged.

He'd just complimented me on my fitness at my age when I humbly told him (between ragged breaths) that I was spent. I said farewell. Dropping off abruptly, I slowed, eventually regained my breath, and headed back to the hotel. It's funny because I wasn't thinking about my breathing that morning until I ran into that strong young runner. Circumstances do that—they force us to look at those elemental functions we take for granted.

As I've aged, I've learned the importance of breathing when it comes to controlling symptoms of stress and anxiety. For example, taking a deep, cleansing breath before responding to an irritating situation can help. A few years back, I learned a trick I call "blowing out the candles." If I'm stressed or anxious, I've learned to hold up my five fingers in front of my face. I then inhale deeply and pretend each finger is a candle, exhaling forcefully to blow them out. The process seems juvenile, but I've found that pausing this way to concentrate on breathing helps me calm down.

It's funny because I wasn't thinking about my breathing that morning until I ran into that strong young runner.

I've also found breathing exercises to be helpful when I can't fall asleep. I'll inhale deeply through my nose to a count of five, then hold my breath for the same amount of time, and follow that with a steady exhale of five seconds. Repeating this pattern helps me to calm down and find sleep.

Permit yourself to slow down and take inventory of your respiratory rate. Through attention and effort, you'll be able to fashion this overlooked function into a useful tool. You may then find that controlled breathing provides extra wind for your sails—or that it lets you catch your breath on a busy day.

CHAPTER 53

IT'S RAINING IN THE OTHER RUNNER'S LANE

People are prone to complain about their circumstances. Some of us fuss more frequently than others. I've succumbed to this condition too many times over the years. I remember complaining bitterly while warming up in the rain for a track meet in early April in Spokane, Washington. It was the early 1980s, and I was preparing to race on an ill-kept cinder track. I knew it was going to be a cold, wet, mud-fest—perfect conditions for a bad race.

I griped to my coach, who looked at me and grinned with wry amusement. He then uttered a phrase I've never forgotten: "Buck up. It's raining in the other runner's lane too." I've thought about those words many times over the years. They come to mind when I'm overly focused on my own circumstances, feelings, or perceived hardships.

So often we think our difficulties are unique. Isolated by self-focus, we fail to recognize the plight of others. We tend to think we're alone in our suffering. But our circumstances aren't singular. Much of what we experience is typical to the human condition. Life is difficult. We all experience hardship—whether running in adverse conditions or not.

While it's true our circumstances are unique and some people do experience more misfortune than others, when it comes to general human conditions, we're all in the same boat.

> **Much of what we experience is typical to the human condition. Life is difficult. We all experience hardship—whether running in adverse conditions or not.**

To quote Judge Holden from *Blood Meridian*, "What is true of one man, is true of many."[121] We do indeed face the same elements as those around us. And yet we tend to overestimate our own difficulties and minimize those of our neighbors.

Over the years I've found Coach's reminder helpful, especially at the beginning of my career as an attorney. When concerned about an upcoming legal proceeding, it helps to remember that opposing counsel faces the same circumstances, just from a different perspective. It's like two sides of the same coin.

We've all heard the saying that life isn't fair. It's a valid observation. Trials and tribulations aren't newcomers on the stage of life. If you need a refresher on the ubiquity of suffering, read a history book and you'll quickly gain perspective. As Solomon put it, "There is nothing new under the sun."[122]

When we find ourselves in a tough spot, we should follow Coach's advice and buck up. Let's try to remember it's also raining in the other person's lane. This image will help us focus outward. The shift of attention can end our ruminating and liberate us from ourselves.

Self-pity isn't useful and, as our perspective changes, we find ourselves in a better place. And once there, we're less likely to complain.

CHAPTER 54

IN THE DARK

We spend a lot time in the dark—literally and figuratively. Being in the dark is a common human experience. Sometimes we are there of our own choice. Other times, darkness is forced on us. Recently I found myself in the latter category at my health club after a short summer run.

I'd just finished a post-run workout inside the club when the power went out. Sweaty and still wearing my running clothes, I headed to the locker room. It was dimly lit by an emergency light. I sat in the hot tub; it was eerily silent. After that, showering was easy but shaving was a challenge. As I peered in the dark mirror, backlit by the flashlight on my cellphone, I realized I looked better in the dark. I managed to knot my tie and emerged blinking in the bright morning air. It was nice to see again. I was reminded that, "Light is sweet. It's wonderful to see the sun!"[123]

I survived the brief power outage ordeal; we call that a "first world problem." Other than missing a few spots on my face when I shaved and emerging with a tie that was slightly askew, no ill befell me that morning. But the experience made me think about lack of light. Darkness is often a metaphor for ignorance. And sometimes we choose to remain in the dark.

Years back, when I was a young attorney, one of the senior partners at my firm would sometimes make an afternoon round to check on the younger lawyers. When he got to my office, he'd invariably flip off the lights and say, "There you go, you're back in the dark—your comfort zone." He was teasing. (I think.) And yet, there was truth in what he was saying. I was an aggressive but inexperienced litigator who often behaved like a bull in a china shop because I hadn't yet learned better. He's since reassured me that I didn't remain in the dark with my lawyering proficiency.

My time as a runner is different. I've willingly entered the dark many times, having run many miles sans sunlight. The days are short during a Minnesota winter and, as a result, most of my runs during this season are in the dark. I love the quiet of an early morning solo winter run. But there's risk. And we're often oblivious to the danger that lurks in the darkness.

Several years back I was running in the pre-dawn hours before work in late February. It was cold, icy, and dark. I was traveling down a snow-cleared sidewalk when I hit an unlit patch of glare ice. Unfortunately, I'd changed direction to go around a corner just as I encountered the ice. Off balance, I couldn't catch myself.

> **I love the quiet of an early morning solo winter run. But there's risk. And we're often oblivious to the danger that lurks in the darkness.**

Down I went, falling to my left. I instinctively tried to break my fall with an outstretched hand. Unfortunately, the only thing that broke was a bone in my wrist. As I lay on the ground, I could now see the ice on which I'd slipped. Too late. Darkness had done its dirty deed.

After that injury, I started wearing a headlamp on dark winter runs. Illuminating the immediate terrain is not only prudent, it's also helpful. I'm not saying you shouldn't run in the dark, but please recognize that you face greater risk of injury when you can't perceive hidden dangers.

This concept is true in all areas of life. How many of us are running around oblivious to our surroundings? Ignorance is not always bliss; it's often dangerous. So be prudent, be aware, and be informed. Feel free to seek enlightenment. Shedding some light on your path may save you from grief.

CHAPTER 55
RUN FAST

According to the old saying, "practice makes perfect." From experience, however, we know that isn't true. We've all likely heard the supposed solution; namely, "perfect practice makes perfect." But we know this version isn't true either, because nobody's perfect. A more accurate rendition is that we tend to perform in the same way we practice. How we've done things before often dictates how we'll do them in the future.

We see this principle at work in the lives of those who perform heroic deeds. There are different theories as to why a person behaves heroically during a crisis. My theory is that the noble act is usually a progression of who the person is and what they've been doing, over time, leading to the defining moment. In other words, it's the result of all the other choices previously made that come to fruition in the crucible—perhaps best described as the culmination of character.

Granted, we've all heard of instances where a person unexpectedly rises to the occasion and behaves admirably in a moment of crisis. Dickens offers a moving example of unforeseen heroism in his classic *A Tale of Two Cities*, when Sydney Carton, a scoundrel, substitutes himself in place of the doomed Charles Darnay. Sydney's words on his way to the guillotine emphasize the unexpected nature of his sacrifice: "It is a far, far better thing that I do, than I have ever done[.]"[124]

His behavior is noble. It takes great love to willingly lay down your life for another.

I suspect however, that those types of unexpected actions are rare. On football, Super Bowl-winning coach Bill Parcells once said, "You are what your record is." Blunt, but on point. This observation suggests that present behavior and character are the natural progression of good choices made over time. In other words, when it comes to self-effort, small decisions accumulate and lead to outcome.

Regardless of past record, sometimes athletes do elevate their game, with the result that they perform better than they've practiced. As Tour de France enthusiasts sometimes say, "The jersey elevates the rider." This happens when a middle-of-the-pack rider unexpectedly finds himself leading the race after a stage.

Thrust into the famed yellow jersey, which signifies the overall leader, this cyclist then outperforms expectations for several stages in an attempt to maintain the lead. It's inspiring when it happens, but it also isn't the norm in the peloton, nor in athletics in general. Rather, as with most activities, past performance is a good indicator of future performance.

I encountered this principle while lifting weights with friends during my college years. We soon learned that if we wanted to advance to heavier lifts, we not only needed to be consistent in our workouts, we also had to get used to handling heavier weight. To do so we'd periodically take turns bench pressing more weight than we could handle, with a spotter on each side helping to lower and then lift the weight, so the lifter could safely work with the increased load. This process accustomed our bodies to the feel of heavier weights.

We see the same concept at work in running. If you want to run fast, you've got to practice running fast. It doesn't matter how old you are or your level of athleticism. If you want to improve your speed, you've got to get used to the discomfort of increased tempo, ragged breath, and pain. Writing to older runners, Hal Higdon says: "Long-distance running at relatively slow paces can only carry you so far. If you want to improve, you need to add speedwork."[125]

If you want to improve your speed, you've got to get used to the discomfort of increased tempo, ragged breath, and pain.

A steady diet of long slow-distance running will maintain your fitness, but it will also make you a slow long-distance runner. Years back I ran with a fellow who'd run fast in high school—much faster than myself. Like all of us in the middle years, he's slowed with time. He still runs a lot of miles, but they're all done at the same slow tempo. As a result, he now has one gear: slow.

If you want to keep running as fast as you can, then periodically practice running fast. I'm not saying you need to do high intensity on a frequent basis, but it's good to periodically blow the carbon out of the pipes. It'll get your blood pumping and allow you to break you out of the doldrums.

And by doing so, you may find you're able to run faster or—age depending—not slow down so quickly. If nothing else, you'll burn more calories in a shorter period and your internal combustion engine will burn more fiercely for several hours afterward.

CHAPTER 56
HOW TO WRECK A DAY

There are many ways to wreck a day. One surefire method is to run much harder than needed. My running buddy and I have "successfully" employed this tactic too many times. These outings usually begin in the guise of an enjoyable, long, slow run. What unfolds however, is a different story. I'd like to say that our pace increases inexplicably. But that wouldn't be true.

There's a competitive element in our relationship that has fueled this dysfunction. The sad result is that we frequently have run too hard. We ruined many Saturdays with our antics. This was foolish behavior. These were training runs that should have been run at an easy to moderate pace. We knew that, but stupid is as stupid does. Reminiscent of a scene from the movie *Dumb and Dumber*, we'd egg each other on toward the inevitable result. And like dogs returning to our vomit, we used to repeat this folly regularly.[126]

Since we usually run in the morning, on those occasions when we ran too hard, the remains of the day were spent in an exhausted mental fog that wouldn't lift. My friend calls this condition a "self-induced transient flu." This semi-catatonic state caused disengagement from our families. Upset by our post-run lethargy, our spouses would criticize our self-centered behavior. Their observations were accurate.

After expending the day's allotted energy on a morning run, our internal fuel tanks were empty. The remainder of the day would crater beneath us despite best intentions. No meaningful activity would be performed; the day would be wrecked. Fortunately, the older we get, the less often we do this. Although I'm not sure that age has made us wiser; rather, I think we're just less ambitious in our middle years.

Proving the apple doesn't fall far from the tree, my father also demonstrated that he knew how to wreck a day with similar behavior. At the time, he'd just become a septuagenarian. He was racing a 10K that he'd run a couple of times before. It was his first race in the 70-year-old bracket. My dad wanted to win his age group and collect some hardware. He knew he'd have to run fast to beat the previous year's winner. So he set an aspirational goal. Intent on setting the old man mark, he delivered a Herculean effort on race day. As he put it, he pushed himself to go hard the entire race.

The good news is that Dad accomplished his goal. He won his age group. In fact, his time would've won multiple younger age groups! The bad news is that he didn't have to run so hard. It turns out the fellow he was worried about didn't even run the race that year. As a result, my old man finished with a margin of several minutes in his bracket. Worse yet, he expended so much energy that, reminiscent of his foolish firstborn, he was spent and worthless for the remainder of the day. As they say, "Like root, like fruit."

Spending more energy than needed is wasteful and unwise. Sometimes we can't accurately measure the output required for a task, but other times we know what's needed. We should be mindful of what a job requires. We don't get credit for extra expenditures.

Certain obligations require more exertion than others. And sometimes we can't tell how much effort is required beforehand. But often we do know, and there is no reason to exceed the energy required to accomplish the task. How does the saying go? Measure twice and cut once. We need to be efficient in our undertakings.

Conservation of resources is wise. If you're purchasing an item that can be acquired for ten dollars, then, in most circumstances, you'd be foolish to pay twenty. Sometimes there's a reason for the extra cost, but that's probably the exception and not the rule.

With so many things in life, avoidance of superfluous behaviors will increase efficiency and provide more margin for your day.

We're all finite creatures. Nobody possesses unlimited resources. If you waste more than is needed on one activity, you'll have less energy for the remaining tasks. Keep this principle in mind and you won't needlessly wreck your day.

CHAPTER 57

DON'T ALWAYS KEEP TRACK

Certain people like to keep track of things. They make lists. Some outline what needs to be done, while others memorialize what has been done.

I understand the to-do list, but why keep a list of accomplishments? The answer could be that many of us seek to justify ourselves by external measurements. Those who fit into this category feel better when we can score tangible results.

I fall into this trap regularly. My running buddy has teased me about this tendency many times over the years. In his words, I'm "the great quantifier." He's convinced I keep a list for everything. He's not too far off the mark. Some of the lists I've compiled over the years:

- miles run across a period of years;
- hours studied in college;
- books read over two decades;
- hours billed per week;
- dollars produced per month;
- cases tried in my career;
  and, yes . . .
- pull-ups.

There are other lists. But I'll stop before my neurotic tendencies overrun the page—you get the point. These tallies suggest a strong need to validate myself. I know I'm not alone in this struggle. Many people keep lists. But those of us who keep track need to be aware of the associated pitfalls.

Memorializing details can drain joy and subvert the purpose for which you did the activity in the first place. When it becomes more about recording another accomplishment as opposed to enjoying what you've done, you probably need to take a break from the list-making.

We see evidence of subversion with the step count craze. While I'm a proponent of fitness, the goal isn't step recordation; rather, the goal is to be active. Step count helps you get there. Many people seem to forget this. A coworker of mine was known on occasion to twirl her arms rapidly in front of herself. I saw her doing this once and asked why her arms were in motion. She told me this action tricks her Fitbit into thinking she is taking steps. That way, if the day was less active, she could still get her desired step count in. I wasn't sure how to respond to that statement, until I thought about my own list-making tendencies. Then I chose to remain silent. To each their own, I suppose.

> **I wasn't sure how to respond to that statement, until I thought about my own list-making tendencies. Then I chose to remain silent.**

So many runners (like me) keep track of pace, distance, weather conditions, heart rate, VO2 max, and other data. Extensive data collection makes sense for some runners depending on circumstances, but it can overly complicate the sport. And if you're always trying to hit some goal, there's going to be dissatisfaction on those days when you don't live up to your desired outcome.

This will sound strange coming from me, but when you go for a run, it's OK to ignore your watch. Those who do enjoy a unique liberty. My wife's Uncle Vince is a great example of a runner who ignored the watch. In fact, he didn't wear one when he ran. One of ten children—and the youngest boy—he was born to Italian immigrants. He grew up in New York and later taught Italian at a high school in Philadelphia for many years before obtaining his Ph.D. and moving to the college ranks. This avuncular fellow is tall, friendly, and hilarious. Conversations with him are never boring.

Uncle Vince took up running later in life. It happened gradually. He used to go for long walks and once, on the way home, he broke into a short jog. Over time he would jog more, and eventually he was running long distances. It's hard to say how far or how fast he ran because he never wore a watch. If you asked him, he'd tell you he ran for about an hour. The freedom with which he enjoyed the sport was refreshing—and rare. There aren't many people like Uncle Vince.

I'm not saying never keep track. There are times when it's useful to record data—especially if you're training for a race or you're an elite runner. But if you're the type who always keeps track, then do yourself a favor and periodically forego the watch.

No Secret Santa is going to review your list or check it twice. Keeping a tally won't make you naughty or nice. Go ahead and give yourself a break.

CHAPTER 58

ON SIMPLICITY

According to Sir Winston Churchill, "All the great things are simple." I suspect he wasn't thinking of running when he made this observation. But using his definition, running is great. The sport is wonderfully simplistic. It doesn't require much preparation or equipment.

Unlike golfers, who may claim that a new set of clubs will improve their game, runners don't harbor illusions that a new pair of shoes will take their performance to the next level. And unlike the cyclist, a flat usually doesn't disrupt a run—unless one stops to help change a tire. The runner need not sharpen nor wax any accessories, and no helmet is required.

The spartan nature of running provides a nice contrast to the complex modern world. One can run just about anywhere. And you don't need a lot of extra gear—just some shoes and adequate attire. In statistics, they call that reducing the variables. Again, keep it simple.

The spartan nature of running provides a nice contrast to the complex modern world.

The simplicity of running can also be seen in its efficiency. While not every runner demonstrates efficient form, the activity is a productive mode of exercise. I was reminded of this aspect when I spent a recent winter nursing an injury, and I often walked the dog on the same routes I used to run. Those walks took twice as long to complete and, once done, I didn't experience the same afterglow I get following a run.

According to Thoreau, our lives are "frittered away by detail" and thus, he urged, "Simplicity, simplicity, simplicity!"[127] His advice is sage but hard to implement. The modern person wears many different hats. It seems that as soon as we simplify one area of life, other complexities crowd in on us.

So while running won't simplify your life, it can provide an otherwise busy day with a simple interlude. And that's a good start.

CHAPTER 59

RUNNING CONNECTS

During my college years, I initially entertained the idea of attending medical school. As a result, I took two years of science classes before deciding I wasn't medical material. In biology, I studied connective tissue, which is the material that joins muscles to bones to allow movement.[128]

Although I don't want to push the analogy too far, running, in its own way, is an organic connector.

Running has connected me to many different people—coaches, teammates, family, and friends. My father and I share a unique bond given the years we spent running together. Our shared activity created a cherished connection. And my wife has often teased me about my "special friendship" with my running buddy—a relationship forged through hours of running.

Over the years, some of the connections have come full circle. My grandparents were there waiting at the finish line of one of my very first races. Fast-forward several decades later and my granddaughter was waiting for me at the finish line of one of my last races.

The sport has connected me with strangers. Running can bridge cultural differences and language barriers. Over the last couple of winters I've done most of my long runs alone on the weekends. While on those solo runs, I'll often run by the same gentleman—sometimes passing him up to three times in one run—as I crisscross the neighborhoods around my house. He's a slight fellow and ambulates slowly. His English is broken but his smile magnificent.

When our paths first crossed, I'd wave. He'd nod and smile in return. After a few more sightings on later runs, I began to call out a greeting. He'd respond in kind. Finally, on one occasion I stopped and shook his hand. Although communication was difficult, we cemented a connection that day. Each time I see him now, I stop and we clasp hands in a warm greeting. This can occur a couple of times during my weekend run. These interactions brighten my day and put a spring in my step. But for running, I never would've connected with this cheerful pedestrian.

Running outside has also connected me to nature. I'm not intending to go all-out Walden Pond here, but logging outdoor miles for several decades has deepened my appreciation for being outdoors. It's also redeemed my perspective on cold winter days. Running through the snow-laden trees during a Minnesota winter provides a unique type of "forest bathing"—an experience the Japanese refer to as *shinrin-yoku*.[129]

> **Running also provides a great connection to places. Going for a run is a favorite activity of mine on vacation. It's an intimate way to explore a new venue.**

Running also provides a great connection to places. Going for a run is a favorite activity of mine on vacation. It's an intimate way to explore a new venue. There's nothing quite like getting your boots on the ground in a new place. Over the years I've run in many different locations, and while many of those daily runs blend together in my mind, here are some vacation runs that stand out:

- a hot and humid Texas run;
- a blustery snow run in the mountains of Montana;
- a windy run on the beach in South Florida;

- a snow-choked run at Lake Okoboji, Iowa;
- a cedar-scented, rain-filled run in Gig Harbor, Washington;
- a run past barking sea lions on California's Monterey Peninsula;
- a dry mountain run in Arizona;
- a rainy run through red clay on the backroads of rural Mississippi;
- a cold and dark hill run in the Port of Duluth, Minnesota; and,
- a magical North Carolina evening run in the Smoky Mountains among wisps of fog.

The list goes on. It's a treasure trove of memories.

Running also connects me to myself. Sometimes I get frazzled and discombobulated. A good hard run allows me to settle down. It grounds me. The activity provides the clarity of mind to regain perspective.

Running has been a conduit that allows me to plug into other areas of life. I find the sport to be an amplifier that intensifies experiences and relationships. I'm grateful for the varied connections it has provided.

CHAPTER 60
DON'T COMPARE

Western culture rests on consumerism. Buying stuff we need isn't bad, but the effects of marketing can be insidious. Advertisements drive consumption by provoking comparison. And comparison often foments dissatisfaction with our current circumstances. We've all heard of the danger of "Keeping up with the Joneses." Simply put, comparison kills contentment. It can put us in a bad place.

We experience more satisfaction if we avoid comparison. Comparing ourselves to others—or viewing present accomplishments through the lens of a past performance—drains our joy. We inevitably come up short when we compare. Someone else is always richer, smarter, skinnier, better-connected, nicer-looking, more accomplished—or faster. For these reasons, we're wise to avoid comparisons. They're a dead end.

Several years back the comparison trap sprung on me while running at the Como Relays. This annual event is held on Wednesday evenings in August in Minnesota's capital city. Teams are comprised of two runners, and members alternate running a set distance until the event is complete. The usual leg is one mile, and the number of miles required increases each week until the last week, at which point each runner runs five one-mile stints. It's a good fitness test. And it's usually hot, muggy, and buggy—classic late summer running in the upper Midwest.

On this steamy night, I remember watching a younger runner who was fast—much faster than me. He flew. His form seemed effortless. I was jealous of his ability and pace. Later that evening I mentioned my envy to my wife, who had been kind enough to bring the kids along to cheer on their old man. She listened and then told me that another runner from a different team had approached her while I was running and commented on how fast I was, with apparent envy. How ironic: here she was sandwiched between two middle-aged fellows who were comparing themselves to another and coming up short.

Self-comparison is just as bad. Some time back I was talking to a friend at my firm after a morning run. He asked how my run had gone. The poor fellow; I unloaded. He received a detailed summary of my effort. It was a Thursday, my perceived "hard day." That means I try to run hard on that day. (Please note my emphasis on the words "perceived" and "try.") That morning, I'd run in what I considered to be a slower gear, but still suffered for most of the outing.

Oversharing my story, I concluded with the observation that I used to be able to run much faster. When I was done, this patient lawyer responded, "Well, at least you can still run." This was meaningful insight. Instead of comparisons to the past, I was reminded that, while almost 50 years old, I was still able to run a reasonable amount. Given that perspective, my focus was adjusted.

> **When I was done, this patient lawyer responded, "Well, at least you can still run."**

The lesson is simple: don't compare. Running is relative. Go ahead and push yourself, but enjoy what you can do. You'll be faster than some and slower than others. And that's OK. Practice putting off comparisons and putting on contentment. The former is a straitjacket that stifles while the latter "is the crown jewel of a happy life."[130]

We do well to remember this: "Contentment is not having what you want, but wanting what you already have."[131]

CHAPTER 61

GRIT IS GOOD

A book about running wouldn't be complete without a discussion on grit. As noted earlier, grit is good. In her book on the subject, Angela Duckworth defines the term as "a combination of passion and perseverance[.]"[132] By grit I don't mean being stubborn to a fault. Being pigheaded isn't a virtue. Rather, I'm talking about the ability to endure and persevere. A close cousin of resilience, grit has to do with toughness.

We all admire grit—stick-to-itiveness, perseverance, the ability to hang in there. Toughness. No matter how you define the term, it's universally admired. It seems too few people genuinely possess a good dose of it.

For some reason, many people overestimate their grittiness. If I had a nickel for every time I heard a client claim they have a high pain threshold, I'd have a bulging money bag. Why do so many misstate their own toughness? Granted, there's no way to measure one's own grit, so perhaps we're better to avoid claims we can't substantiate.

Although we can't measure grit, we do recognize it when we see it demonstrated in others. Two examples of great grit came to mind while pondering this subject. The first is my daughter, Kate. Earlier in this book I discussed her brain injury. Following graduation from college, she moved to Mississippi to train horses. Shortly after the move she was injured while breaking a colt; the resulting head trauma put her in a coma.

Her recovery was miraculous. It was also propelled by her grit. Watching her relearn how to talk, walk, and eventually run—with no complaints—was inspiring. She tackled her disability head on. She worked hard. Her tenacious character glowed brightly in the aftermath of her accident.

> **Her recovery was miraculous. It was also propelled by her grit. Watching her relearn how to talk, walk, and eventually run—with no complaints— was inspiring.**

Another Minnesotan, Gabriele Grunewald, demonstrated similar grittiness in a long battle with cancer. A walk-on with the track team at the University of Minnesota, she ultimately became an all-American in the 1500 meters even though she was battling cancer.[133] She raced her way through multiple bouts with cancer and eventually became a professional athlete. A US indoor national champ in the 3000 meters, she later missed qualifying for the Olympics by one spot. She was easy to spot on the track given the thirteen-inch scar on her abdomen, a mark she considered "a sign of her ability to handle adversity."[134] Cancer eventually got the upper hand when she died at 32, but she battled ferociously until the end.

Watching or hearing stories about others who've battled through adversity provides tremendous inspiration to the rest of us. And while some people, like Kate and Gabriele, appear to possess more inherent grit than others, we can all learn from their example. Grit is like a muscle. The more we exercise it, the stronger it gets. As the famous preacher Charles Spurgeon once noted, "It is only by enduring that we learn to endure."[135]

Possessing grit won't make you a better person, and it won't necessarily make you a better runner. But it will allow you to endure hardship and difficulties that are invariably encountered along the way. As we move through life, let's remember the words of Saint Paul, who encouraged us to run the race set before us with endurance, keeping our eyes on the prize.[136] May we stay the course.

THE FINAL LAP

I finished the draft of this book in the late fall, a fitting season for conclusion. It's a time when Minnesota farmers are working hard to bring in the last of the harvest. As I composed these words in my mind on a dark, chilly, fall run, my thoughts were interrupted by a blast of wind that sent dried and fallen leaves into sudden motion. Hearing those leaves scuttle by, I turned and watched them disappear into the darkness behind me.

The image of those disappearing leaves wasn't lost on me; they were like yesterday's miles receding into the past. But unlike those fallen leaves that hurried off into forgotten places, the miles I've run have accumulated in my mind. Stored up in my mental warehouse, the individual miles combine to form a rich repository of memory and experience.

Looking back across four decades of running, I marvel at the wide curriculum the activity has provided me. I won't claim that running taught me everything I needed to know; that would be a stretch. My life has been full of other great instructors as well. That said, running has been an excellent teacher, and I've learned a lot of useful lessons during the miles spent under its tutelage.

The lessons learned from running vary—they span a wide gamut from recreation to rest, relationship to retreat, reflection to resilience. It's all there. The

The sport embodies life. That's because running is a metaphor for life. Like life itself, running requires engagement.

sport embodies life. That's because running is a metaphor for life. Like life itself, running requires engagement—and the more you engage, the more you receive in return. And when you do embrace the sport, you'll find this life tutor to be both affordable and accessible.

Although my writing on the subject has come to an end, I know I haven't yet learned all that running has to teach. For, as Tolkien wrote, "the Road goes ever on and on."[137]

As I continue to travel my road, I'm confident there will be new lessons to be learned while on the run.

EPILOGUE
A RUNNING TALE

A long time ago, in a land far, far away, there was a tiny kingdom known as the Inland Empire. The capital of this land was known as Spokane. This proud city wasn't surrounded by a moat, but it did have a nice river flowing through the center of town.

The inhabitants of this place took their running seriously.

Years earlier, a former Olympian named Don Kardong had established an annual tradition called the Bloomsday Race. This yearly event was held during the Lilac Festival, and throngs of well-wishers would line the storied course to cheer on the participants.

At that time there lived in the city of Spokane a knight of small renown. Although his retinue was small, this hardy warrior had proven himself faithful in the service of the King. This knight sired four children, the eldest of whom was a boy of about ten at the time our story begins. This youngster, like many fellows his age, spent much time fishing in the river, reading books, and playing games with friends.

One day it came into the knight's head that he should train the firstborn so he too could participate in the fine tradition of the Bloomsday Race. The lad was reluctant at first, but eventually he accepted the offer. Training runs involved no enchantment; rather, they produced many tears and bitter complaints as the youth lagged behind his father. The boy would often ask if he could quit running and return home. At these times the father would stop and wait for him, reminding his son, "We are in this together."

When his father admonished the lad about the need to properly train to cover the distance, the boy laughed and made excuses. The knight reminded his young charge that the race was long and its mighty hill had broken the heart and will of many a fine runner. This dreaded obstacle rose steeply out of the ground at about the sixth mile on the course. It continued on for some time.

The foolish child laughed off his father's advice and responded whimsically, "Oh Father, it won't be hard for me to go up the hill. I'll just skip." The knight gently shook his head and tried to disabuse his young charge of this silly notion, but to no avail. Instead, the boy's sporadic training continued until the day of the great race.

On race day the rosy fingers of dawn gently parted the night sky and gave way to a beautiful spring morning. Birds chirped merrily. The air was redolent with the smell of lilacs. Arriving early at the starting line, the knight and his boy tucked themselves into the middle of the crowd and, after hearing the gun, commenced to run. For a while, it was good fun.

Things went well for the first several miles. Surprised by his son's unexpected strength, the father reveled in the event. Soon, however, the knight noticed he was having difficulty keeping up with the spritely lad. The pair continued along until the shadow of the hill loomed large over them.

As the two began their ascent up the legendary incline, it was clear the knight could no longer keep pace with his son. Not wanting to hold him back, he encouraged his young charge. "Go ahead, son. Go on. Go for it," he yelled. Heeding this encouragement, the boy took off. The father watched the youngster accelerate and fly up the hill. He soon lost sight of his firstborn amid the crowded field. The knight felt both joy and sadness at the parting.

The knight trudged his way to the top of the hill. He didn't feel good. The hill seemed longer than he remembered. When he finally reached the crown, he was mightily discouraged. He took a few deep breaths and attempted to top off the hill when he noticed, to his surprise, his son standing about 100 yards ahead, looking expectantly back in his direction.

The knight excitedly called out the child's name. The boy's face brightened, and he ran back toward his father. As the lad drew near, his father asked what was wrong. The boy replied, "Dad, we're in this together."

The joy of the reunion wasn't lost on the knight. They finished the race together. Afterward, there was much celebrating.

The knight never forgot that day with his boy. Legend says the story became a staple sermon illustration in the decades that followed. Eyewitnesses report the race left an indelible mark on the boy as well, and that as he came of age, he sought to faithfully serve his King—just like his father.

And to this day that former lad still loves to run—just not skip—up hills.

It has also been said that some running stories take on mythic proportions. Perhaps like tales of old, they grow taller with the passage of time. These stories may take on a life of their own, but they also can serve to encourage and inspire others. If nothing else, this story shows that life lessons can indeed be learned on the run.

NOTES

1. V. Raymond Edman, *Storms and Starlight* (Wheaton, IL: Van Kempen Press, 1951), p. 10.

2. Emma Lazarus, "The New Colossus," *The Statue of Liberty* (New York, NY, 1883).

3. Stephen Crane, *The Red Badge of Courage* (Pleasantville, NY: The Readers Digest Association, Inc., originally 1895, reproduced 1982), p. 52.

4. American Bar Association, "Report from the National Task Force on Lawyer Well-Being," Nov. 9, 2018, available at www.americanbar.org/groups/lawyer_assistance/task_force_report/.

5. Winston Churchill, *Painting as a Pastime* (New York, NY: Cornerstone Library Publications, 1965), p. 7.

6. *Chariots of Fire*, Hugh Hudson, director (London, UK: Enigma Productions, 1981).

7. Tim Noakes, M.D., *Lore of Running*, 4th Edition (Oxford University Press USA, 2001, 2003), p. 919.

8. *The Sound of Music*, Robert Wise, director (Hollywood, CA: Twentieth Century Fox, 1965).

9. Gretchen Rubin, *Better Than Before* (New York, NY: Crown Publishers, 2015), p. 79.

10. Ecclesiastes 9:11, NLT.

11. Edward Stafford, "An Afternoon with Hemingway," *Writer's Digest* magazine, originally published September 1961, available at https://www.writersdigest.com/writing-articles/by-writing-genre/literary-fiction-by-writing-genre/an_interview_with_hemingway.

12. James 4:14, NKJV.

13. Proverbs 18:21, HCSB.

14. T. S. Eliot, "The Waste Land," from *The Complete Poems and Plays 1909-1950* (New York, NY: Harcourt, Brace & World, Inc., 1966), p. 37.

15. Charles Dickens, *A Tale of Two Cities* (New York: Barnes & Noble Books, originally 1859, repr. 2004,), p. 7.

16. David Kempston, *That's Why They Call It Practicing Law* (Lexington, KY: Amazon, 2017), p. 45.

17. "oxygen debt," *Merriam-Webster.com*, 2019, https://www.merriam-webster.com/dictionary./oxygen%20debt.

18. Neal Bascomb, *The Perfect Mile* (New York, NY: Houghton Mifflin, 2005), p. 189.

19. Thomas Stanley, *The Millionaire Next Door* (New York, NY: Pocket Books, 1996), p. 161.

20. Richard Peck, *A Year Down Yonder* (New York, NY: Puffin Books, 2000), p. 12.

21. Proverbs 12:23, NIV.

22. William Shakespeare, *Hamlet*, Act 1, Scene 3, Line 68.

23. Shelby Foote, *The Civil War: A Narrative: Volume 1: Fort Sumter to Perryville* (New York, NY; Random House, originally 1958, repr. 1986), p. 430.

24. Luke 12:15, NLT.

25. Ray Pritchard, *The ABC's of Wisdom: Building Character with Solomon* (Chicago, IL: Moody Press, 1997) p. 42.

26. John Keats, "Ode on a Grecian Urn," *Romantic Poets* (New York, NY: The Colonial Press, originally 1950, repr. 1961), p. 385.

27. Dylan Thomas, "Do Not Go Gentle Into That Good Night," *The Norton Anthology of Modern Poetry*, 2nd Edition, (New York, NY: W. W. Norton & Company, originally 1973, repr. 1988), p. 927.

28. Matthew 7:12, NASB.

29. Mark Divine, *The Way of the Seal* (White Plains, NY: Reader's Digest Adult Trade Publishing, 2013), p. 9.

30. Richard Swenson, M.D., *Margin* (Colorado Springs, CO: NavPress, 2004) p. 36.

31. Quoted in L. B. Cowman, *Streams in the Desert* (Grand Rapids, MI: Zondervan, originally 1925, repr. 1997), p. 43.

32. Hal Higden, *Masters Running* (New York, NY: Rodale, 2005), p. 38.

33. Ibid., 15.

34. Genesis 2:3, NIV.

35. Swenson, *Margin*, 100.

36. Cormac McCarthy, *The Road* (New York, NY: Alfred A. Knopf, 2006), pp. 196, 197.

37. Ray Stedman, *The Practice of His Presence* (Grand Rapids, MI: Discovery House Publishing, 2006), p. 102.

38. 2 Samuel 12:7, ESV.

39. Matthew 19:5, NASB.

40. Margaret George, *Elizabeth I* (New York, NY: Viking Press, 2011), p. 639.

41. 1 Corinthians 15:43, 50, NLT.

42. Proverbs 16:20, NLT.

43. Percy Bysshe Shelley, "Ozymandias," *Poet's Corner*, Elizabeth Longford (London: Chapmans Publishers Limited, 1992), p. 122.

44. *Megamind*, Tom McGrath, director (Glendale, CA: Dreamworks Animation, 2010).

45. Kenny Moore, *Bowerman and the Men of Oregon* (New York, NY: Rodale, 2006), p. 331.

46. "dissipate," *Merriam-Webster.com*, 2019, available at https://www.merriam-webster.com/dictionary./dissipate.

47. Proverbs 22:3, NLT.

48. Paul Glendinning, *Math in Minutes* (New York, NY: Quercus Publishing, 2014), p. 114.

49. Charles Spurgeon, *Morning and Evening* (Wheaton, IL: Crossway, originally 1865, repr. 2003), January 31.

50. C. S. Lewis, *The Abolition of Man* (New York, NY: HarperCollins Publishers, originally 1944, repr. 2001), p. 18.

51. Meb Keflezighi, *Meb for Mortals* (New York, NY: Rodale, 2015), p. 2.

52. Henri Nouwen, *Reaching Out* (Garden City, NY: Double Day & Company, Inc., 1975), p. 37.

53. Hebrews 13:2, KJV.

54. William Shakespeare, *As You Like It*, Act 2, Scene 7, Line 139.

55. Edman, *Storms and Starlight*, 33.

56. Alan Sillitoe, *The Loneliness of the Long-Distance Runner* (New York, NY: Penguin Group, originally 1959, repr. 1992).

57. Ibid., 19.

58. Ibid., 48.

59. Ibid., 51.

60. Ibid., 43.

61. John Piper, *Why I Love the Apostle Paul* (Wheaton, IL: Crossway, 2019), p. 147.

62. Matthew 21:1-9, ESV.

63. William Wordsworth, "Daffodils," *Favorite Poems Old and New*, Helen Ferris (New York, NY: Bantam Doubleday Dell Publishing Group, Inc., 1957), p. 218.

64. Ibid.

65. Hebrews 12:1, 2, KJV.

66. Kevin Lynch, "Seattle Seahawks fans 'cause minor earthquake' with world record crowd roar," guinnessworldrecords.com, December 4, 2013, available at https://www.

guinnessworldrecords.com/amp/news/2013/12/seattle-seahawks-fans-cause-minor-earthquake-with-world-record-roar-53285/.

67. Pritchard, *The ABC's of Wisdom*, 263.

68. Phil Knight, *Shoe Dog* (New York, NY: Scribner 2016), p. 61.

69. Ibid., 270.

70. C. S. Lewis, *The Four Loves* (New York, NY: Harcourt Brace Jovanovich, Publishers, 1960), p. 92.

71. Ecclesiastes 3:1, NIV.

72. Henry Rono, *Olympic Dream* (Bloomington, IN: AuthorHouse, 2010), pp. 79-85.

73. Ibid., 82, 85.

74. M. Scott Peck, *The Road Less Traveled* (New York, NY: Simon & Schuster, originally 1978, repr. 2003), p. 15.

75. Josh Waitzkin, *The Art of Learning* (New York, NY: Free Press, 2007), p. 44.

76. H. W. Fowler and R. W. Burchfield, *Fowler's Modern English Usage* (Oxford, UK: Oxford University Press, 2004), p. 745.

77. As near as I can tell, this quote is misattribution to Sun Tzu. I reached this conclusion after reviewing four different translations of *The Art of War*. I couldn't find this quote in any of the translations I reviewed, although I frequently saw it cited on the Internet. If any reader discovers otherwise, I'm happy to amend my conclusion.

78. Proverbs 22:23, NLT.

79. Barry Smyth, "Fast Starters and Slow Finishers: A large-scale data analysis of pacing at the beginning and end of the marathon for recreational runners," *Journal of Sports Analytics*, vol. 4, no. 3, pp. 229-242, 2018, available at https://content.iospress.com/articles/journal-of-sports-analytics/jsa205.

80. Angela Duckworth, *Grit* (New York, NY: Scribner, 2016), p. 474.

81. C. S. Lewis, *The Problem of Pain* (New York, NY: HarperCollins Publishers, originally 1940, repr. 2001), p. 91.

82. Divine, *The Way of the Seal*, 107.

83. Ibid.

84. Proverbs 27:2, RSV.

85. J. R. R. Tolkien, *The Two Towers* (New York, NY: Houghton Mifflin Company, originally 1954, repr. 1994), p. 698.

86. Ibid., 673, 674.

87. W. A. Dorland. *Dorland's Illustrated Medical Dictionary*, 27th Ed. (Philadelphia, PA: W. B. Saunders Company, 1988), p. 1196.

88. Donald Venes, Thomas Clayton, and Clarence Taber. *Taber's Cyclopedic Medical Dictionary* (Philadelphia, PA: F. A. Davis Company 2001), p. 316.

89. Thomas Stedman. *Stedman's Medical Dictionary* 28th Ed. (Philadelphia, PA: Lippincott Williams & Wilkins, 2006), p. 2033.

90. Matthew 7:3-5, NLT.

91. E. B. White, *Charlotte's Web* (New York, NY: Barnes & Noble Books, originally 1952, repr. 1997), p. 75.

92. Franz Kafka, "Investigations of a Dog," from *The Complete Stories* (New York, NY: Schocken Books, originally 1931, repr. 1971), p. 303.

93. William Packard, *The Art of Poetry Writing* (New York, NY: St. Martin's Press, 1992), p. 216.

94. Walter Isaacson, *Steve Jobs* (New York, NY: Simon & Schuster, 2011), p. xvii.

95. Ibid., 325.

96. Paul Farfard, "How and Why Lakes Stratify and Turn Over: We explain the science behind the phenomena," International Institute for Sustainable Development, May 18, 2018, available

at https://iisd.org/ela/blog/commentary/lakes-stratify-turn-explain-science-behind-phenomena/.

97. Luke 12:2, NLT.

98. C. S. Lewis, "The Last Battle." From *The Complete Chronicles of Narnia* (New York, NY: HarperCollins Publishers Ltd., originally 1956, repr. 2008), p. 520.

99. "shoot oneself in the foot," Grammarist.com, 2019, available at https://grammarist.com/idiom/shoot-oneself-in-the-foot/.

100. W. A. Dorland. *Dorland's Pocket Medical Dictionary*, 21st Ed. (Philadelphia, PA: W. B. Saunders Company, 1968), p. 318.

101. I Corinthians 9:25, AMP.

102. Robert Martichenko, *Everything I Know About Lean I Learned in First Grade* (Cambridge, MA: The Lean Enterprise Institute, 2008), p. 39.

103. Matt Plummer and Jo Wilson, "The Lie That Perfectionists Tell Themselves," *Harvard Business Review*, May 4, 2018, available at https://hbr.org/2018/05/the-lie-that-perfectionists-tell-themselves.

104. Moore, *Bowerman and the Men of Oregon*, 323.

105. "Billy Graham Trivia: What Is Life's Greatest Surprise?" Billy Graham Evangelistic Society, March 27, 2017, available at https://billygraham.org/story/billy-graham-trivia-lifes-greatest-surprise/.

106. Dale Carnegie, *How to Win Friends and Influence People.* (New York, NY: Simon & Schuster, originally 1936, repr. 1964), p. 189.

107. *Nacho Libre*, Jared Hess, director (Hollywood, CA: Paramount Pictures, 2006).

108. Keflezighi, *Meb for Mortals*, 2.

109. Scott Adams, *How to Fail at Almost Everything and Still Win Big* (New York, NY: Penguin Group, 2013), p. 32.

110. Ibid.

111. Noakes, *Lore of Running*, 301, 302.

112. V. Raymond Edman, *The Disciplines of Life* (Minneapolis, MN: World Wide Publications, 1948), p. 213.

113. Proverbs 17:3, ESV.

114. William Blake, "The Tyger," from *A Treasury of Great Poems English and American*, Louis Untermeyer (New York, NY: Simon and Schuster, 1942), p. 603.

115. Keflezighi, *Meb For Mortals*, 73.

116. Tom Jordan, *Pre* (New York, NY: Rodale, originally 1977, repr. 1997), p. 58.

117. *Free Solo*, Elizabeth Chai Vasarhelyi and Jimmy Chin, directors (Washington, DC: National Geographic Partners, 2018).

118. Edman, *Storms*, 119.

119. "Vital Signs." my.clevelandclinic.org, Cleveland Clinic, 2019, available at https://my.clevelandclinic.org/health/articles/10881-vital-signs.

120. "Respiratory Responses to Exercise." ptdirect.com, PT Direct, 2019, available at https://www.ptdirect.com/training-design/anatomy-and-physiology./acute-respiratory-responses.

121. Cormac McCarthy, *Blood Meridian* (London, UK: Picador, originally 1985, repr. 2011), p. 153.

122. Ecclesiastes 1:9, NIV.

123. Ecclesiastes 11:7, NLT.

124. Dickens, *A Tale of Two Cities*, 372.

125. Higdon, *Masters Running*, 102.

126. Proverbs 26:11, NLT.

127. Henry David Thoreau, *Where I Lived, and What I lived For* (New York; NY: Penguin Group, originally 1924, repr. 2006), p. 69.

128. Rene Fester Kratz, Ph.D., *Biology for Dummies*, 3rd Ed. (Hoboken, NJ: John Wiley & Sons, Inc., 2017), p. 44.

129. Qing Li, M.D., Ph.D., "'Forest Bathing' Is Great for Your Health. Here's How to Do It," Time, May 2, 2018, available at https://time.com/5259602/japanese-forest-bathing/.

130. Charles Spurgeon, *Flowers from a Puritan's Garden*, (Harrisburg, VA: Sprinkle Publications, originally 1883, repr. 1997), p. 141.

131. Pritchard, *The ABC's of Wisdom*, 62.

132. Duckworth, *Grit*, 8.

133. Lindsay Crouse, "Gabriele Grunewald, Runner Who Chronicled Journey with Cancer, Dies at 32," *New York Times*, June 12, 2019, available at http://www.nytimes.com/2019/0/6/12/sports/gabriele-grunewald-dead.html.

134. Ibid.

135. Charles Spurgeon, *Cheque Book of the Bank of Faith* (Ross-shire, Scotland; Christian Focus Publications, 1996, 2007), p. 264.

136. Hebrews 12:2, ESV.

137. J. R. R. Tolkien, *The Fellowship of The Ring* (New York, NY: Ballantine Books, originally 1954, repr. 1999), p. 102.